British Rail Passenger Trains

Roger Wood

Capital Transport

First published 1993

ISBN 185414 152 X

Published by Capital Transport Publishing
38 Long Elmes, Harrow Weald, Middlesex

Printed by The KPC Group, Ashford, Kent

© Roger Wood and Capital Transport Publishing 1993

The cover photographs are by Brian Morrison and Capital Transport

CONTENTS

INTRODUCTION

The British Railways Board administers three passenger service businesses, officially termed Sectors. InterCity operates all long distance main line services centred on London and Birmingham with limited stops and the Gatwick Express between London and the airport. Network SouthEast has responsibility for all other services within a nominal 80 mile radius of London and Regional Railways (previously known as Provincial) runs the remaining local and cross-country services throughout Great Britain.

This book provides extensive coverage of the locomotives and rolling stock owned by each business and the duties on which they are regularly engaged. There are always occasional exceptions and non-scheduled operations under special circumstances. Non-passenger-carrying non-driving vehicles are not included nor locomotives owned solely for infrastructure duties. Similarly, sister locomotives owned by other businesses, particularly Rail express systems (Parcels group), may be borrowed for emergencies or relief duties generally too varied to detail here.

Many non-InterCity services are supported by central government and local authorities. In the case of the seven metropolitan authorities – Strathclyde, Tyne and Wear, Greater Manchester, Merseyside, West Yorkshire, South Yorkshire and West Midlands the Passenger Transport Executive determines with BR Regional Railways the service to be operated and fares charged. Other local authorities usually provide support for services and infrastructure.

Stagecoach Rail became the first private business to enter into an operating franchise for a passenger carrying service with BR in May 1992 with InterCity providing Mk2d Nightrider coaches on London–Aberdeen sleeping car trains. Vehicles were part of BR's standard fleet with the interior fittings adapted to

Stagecoach's specification. Regrettably the venture was unsuccessful and the franchise ceased at the end of October. InterCity has resumed the marketing of seating on this service. Whilst more such operations would appear to be Government policy (shown in the White Paper published in July 1992) and various possible operators, including current BR business management teams, have shown interest for particular services no other franchise has yet been granted. At the time of writing BR's proposed charges for use of infrastructure (track, signalling, stations etc) appear to be causing concern to possible operators.

The information contained herein is believed correct at the time of going to press. For a variety of reasons BR makes small adjustments to the area of operation each week, slightly greater alterations at eight-week intervals and significant changes at the mid-May and end-September timetable changes. Fleet sizes shown are those currently in operating stock or on order, as the context indicates.

All stock receives periodic overhauls dependent on hours in service and/or mileage; most of this routine work is carried out by British Rail Maintenance Ltd (BRML) or British Rail Level 5 Group (L5) depots. Those sites relevant to this publication are BRML Doncaster for diesel locomotive overhauls except Class 43 where it only overhauls the bogies fitted during overhaul at Neville Hill (Leeds) and Bath Road (Bristol) L5 depots. InterCity electric locomotives are overhauled at BRML Doncaster and Springburn (Glasgow). Class 73 electro-diesel locomotives are overhauled at Selhurst L5 depot but will be relocated from April 1993. The diminishing number of conventional 1960s diesel multiple units visit BRML Doncaster for specialist attention. BRML Eastleigh Works plays a supporting role for a few Network SouthEast units, including the diesel-electric fleet. The second generation units have not yet required major overhauls in the accepted sense. Cardiff Canton and Haymarket (Edinburgh) BR Level 4 depots carry out routine bogie changes whilst BRML Doncaster generally carries out the bogie and wheelset changes necessary on fleets based elsewhere in England. English based AC electric multiple units are mainly overhauled at BRML Wolverton (Milton Keynes) with BRML Eastleigh, BR Selhurst and Ilford L5 depots carrying out some lesser overhauls. ScotRail units are overhauled at BRML Springburn. Merseyrail's DC EMUs are given significant attention at Birkenhead depot. The NSE South DC EMUs receive major attention at BRML Eastleigh and intermediate overhauls at Chart Leacon (Ashford), and Selhurst BR L5 depots. Selhurst is scheduled for closure by mid-1993 as new trains have reduced the need for repair facilities. BRML Wolverton has the main role in Hauled Coaching Stock with Springburn and Eastleigh, whilst required by NSE, taking a smaller number.

The first Networker Class 465 EMUs were handed over in December 1991 by BREL York and GEC Metro-Cammell, Birmingham. The first units entered service late November 1992. The first Class 323 unit assembled by Hunslet TPL, Leeds, was delivered at the end of September and taken to BRB Research Engineering Development Unit for extensive type approval tests. Entry into service on Birmingham CrossCity line duties is due in the spring of 1993.

In September BREL was renamed ABB Transportation Ltd. (Asea Brown Boveri) after its parent company. The company is now concerned mainly with new construction, refurbishment and modification work and some component overhauls.

Thanks are due to photographers Robert Casselden, Colin Marsden, Brian Morrison, Barry Nicolle and Bill Wilson for illustrations through this book, and to Brian Aylott for his considerable help with the editorial content.

Roger Wood, January 1993.

INTERCITY

East Coast Main Line

InterCity's flagship train, the 'IC225' operates the majority of services on this route between King's Cross (London) and Edinburgh Waverley. The fleet of 31 trains is booked to be formed of a Class 91 locomotive and a rake of ten Mk4 coaches, including a Driving Van Trailer (DVT) which allows trains to operate with the unmanned locomotive pushing from the rear. The '225' figure indicates the maximum permitted speed of 225km/hr (140mph) although signalling constraints currently limit trains to 125mph in normal traffic. However a 450-mile journey in under four hours, including stops at York and Newcastle, compares well with alternative forms of travel.

Some services are extended to Glasgow Central via Motherwell and forming a convenient alternative route for London passengers and through express services for customers from other east coast locations. These train sets also form most services between King's Cross and Leeds and, until last summer, had been diesel hauled between Leeds and Bradford Forster Square. However this has been suspended while the route is electrified and InterCity 125 High Speed Trains now again work the through London–Bradford services.

The Mk4 sets are booked to be formed Class 91 locomotive, AI2, four AC2, AL2, AJ1, two AD1, NZ5. Six Pullman sets have an extra AD1 and one less AC2 and are booked to diagrams for services where a high First Class business use is normal. All locomotives and coaches are maintained at Bounds Green depot, north London, although limited facilities are available at Edinburgh Craigentinny, Heaton (Newcastle) and Neville Hill (Leeds) depots for cleaning and minor repairs.

In addition to the Bradford service the IC125s, InterCity's former flagship, still ply this route between London and Edinburgh to continue forward to Dundee and Aberdeen, also Perth and Inverness. Very limited services also operate between London and Cleethorpes via Newark (to cease next May), Harrogate and Hull, primarily for the business customer requiring a day in the capital. Eleven IC125 train sets are each formed of eight coaches – GJ2, four GH2, GK1 and two GH1 with a Class 43 power car (locomotive) at each end. The Class 43s are maintained at Neville Hill, the coaches at Craigentinny.

The Cross Country business operates other InterCity services between Leeds, York and Scotland. InterCity's Charter business operates special services over the East Coast route and also allows its air conditioned Mk2d coaches to be 'borrowed' for relief services and other emergencies. Charter does not have use of Class 91s and Mk4s.

The limit of NSE's commuter area is officially Huntingdon, but their services continue the 17 miles to Peterborough by arrangement with InterCity.

West Coast Main Line

This route centres on Euston (London) as a terminus and out through the suburbs past Watford and Milton Keynes, by-passing the NSE extremity of Northampton, to Rugby. Here the first divide in the route allows trains to travel west to Birmingham International, Birmingham New Street and Wolverhampton. A short distance north of Wolverhampton is Oxley Coaching Stock depot, responsible for maintenance of stock used on this service. The inter-city business on this line is very substantial and the London–Birmingham peak period service expanded to 15min intervals from May 1992, when for the first time Pullman services were formed entirely of Mk3 stock. The three sets comprise an NZ5 (DVT), AE1H, two AD1G, AJ1G and five AC2G. The slightly older Mk2f stock continues on other services, formed NZ5, three AD1F, AJ1G and five AC2F.

Although an important junction, local business from Rugby does not warrant many InterCity services calling. It is well served by joint Network SouthEast and Regional Railways EMU services. The main line north serves Nuneaton, Tamworth, Lichfield Trent Valley and Stafford; subsequently the route to Manchester via Stoke on Trent diverges. The main West Coast route continues to Crewe. Crewe's junction with so many routes is the reason most services call there rather than the Cheshire town's own business. Crewe is still the busiest railway centre outside London with two important traction maintenance depots, one for diesel and one for electric locomotives. ABB Transportation (BREL) still has its much reduced engineering works in the town where many of today's locomotives were built (the last in March 1991) and overhauled. The freight yards at Basford Hall, south of the station, handle a busy Freightliner traffic remarshalling trains to pre-planned formations for a variety of destinations.

At Crewe, three InterCity routes leave the London–Scotland line; one to industrial Merseyside for Runcorn and Liverpool Lime Street; another to Stockport and Manchester Piccadilly, the third along the North Wales coast to Holyhead. Liverpool's Edge Hill depot, whilst InterCity owned, is only concerned for WCML with overnight servicing of the Wembley-based trainsets. The service between London and Manchester has two main routes and is positioned to provide a greater business than Liverpool, hence Manchester's Longsight Coaching Stock depot shares full maintenance responsibility for the London route trainsets, although it currently also plays an important role in the Cross Country business. The two traction maintenance depots at Longsight play only a minor role in West Coast operations. The non-electrified North Wales line is 'owned' by Regional Railways North West and limited to three InterCity 125 trains each way daily between Holyhead and Euston. The stock is the same as used on Great Western main line services and is maintained at Laira, Plymouth depot. Whilst three sets, including six Class 43 power cars, are allocated to the route; dedication is not practised. At other times Regional Railways provides connections at Crewe to/from North Wales.

The main route north passes Warrington and Wigan on the way to Preston, and up Shap bank past the Lake District to Carlisle, then Beattock bank through Carstairs and Motherwell to Glasgow Central. InterCity withdrew the through service to Blackpool North on economic grounds from the end of the summer timetable period. Regional Railways operates a regular service over its branch from Preston to the Lancashire coast.

From May 1992 West Coast route maintenance resources were again rearranged. At the London end Wembley depot has ten day service sets of Mk3 stock formed NZ5, two AD1G, AJ1G, five AC2G to operate primarily Liverpool, Manchester, Preston and Carlisle duties. Two similar sets are formed for the Lancashire Pullman, now routed to Preston and Lancaster, with the better seating of AD1H (Mk3b) First Class coaches. Five other sets each have three AD1H coaches, and one set with three AD1G as cover, to form 'Super Pullmans' providing full at-seat dining facilities for First Class passengers at appropriate times on the London–Liverpool/Manchester services, other accommodation is Mk3a specification. In Standard Class, next to the Restaurant Car (AJ1G) the allocated coach includes facilities for wheelchair customers, although very few are advised by BR as having suitably adapted toilets.

Wembley depot also now maintains the sleeping car stock on this route. Two sets have to be allocated to each service, one each way per night, with a spare set formed for maintenance and further vehicles to cover for heavy repairs at depot or main works. Sleeper coaches are now technically unclassified stock, when used for First Class use an upper berth in each two-berth compartment is folded away.

Sets on all but the Fort William service include a 26-seat lounge providing night-caps of hot and cold drinks, including alcohol, and light breakfast. The short Fort William sleeper/Motorail service has a standard First Open coach modified to provide a limited light refreshment service. Cabin stewards, each usually responsible for two sleeper coaches, provide early calls with tea/coffee and biscuits prepared in the Pantry (AU4G) vehicles. The Inverness trains have to run with eight instead of the normal nine sleeper coaches, as they now run north of Edinburgh with a Mk1 parcels van converted to generate power to the train. The pair of Class 37 locomotives allocated to provide traction are not suitably equipped and the high overall cost of a Class 47/4 for just one up and down service daily is not viable. The Inverness station platform capacity causes the restriction to the train's length. During the off-peak winter period the full train can run as it is combined with the Fort William service as far as Edinburgh. The Fort William service sometimes operates in conjunction with a Land Cruise Charter service for the West Highlands.

The sleeper service market is diminishing as the main demand has been the business traveller between London and Scotland and speeds of day trains now provide a through service from London to Aberdeen at 16.00 and later trains with an en-route change. Glasgow and Edinburgh customers have a service from London as late as 18.30 and Newcastle no longer justifies a sleeper with day services hourly from London until 22.00. All London sleeping car services thus use the West Coast route and serve Aberdeen, Edinburgh, Glasgow and Inverness with a short section also serving Fort William line stations. InterCity dropped sleeping accommodation from all except its Glasgow services from May but at the last minute an arrangement was made with a private company, Stagecoach Rail, part of the Stagecoach Holdings coach group, who leased stock and arranged with InterCity for exclusive operation of two coaches on the nightly service to and from Aberdeen. The independent venture was not successful, but InterCity is continuing to provide the facility without the pre-booking that Stagecoach required. Stagecoach operates a linking road coach service between Edinburgh, Perth and Inverness.

The Aberdeen, Edinburgh, Inverness and Fort William sleeper services also include a Motorail facility with cars conveyed by the same train in closed vans. Another Motorail service from Euston is to Carlisle and Edinburgh. Outward jour-neys are Monday to Saturday mornings and Saturday evening, return journeys every afternoon. The Aberdeen service has six sleepers, AS4G and AU4G, AN1F, three sleepers, NH5 (brake van), two AC2D, three NX5 Motorail vans. The Edinburgh sleeper is similarly formed but without the AC2Ds and with five NX5 vans. The Inverness service comprises six AS4G/AU4G, AN1F, AS4G, AU4G, NH5, four NX5 with an AX5 generator coach on the leading end between Inverness and Edinburgh only. The Fort William service comprises an NH5 (brake van), AE2F, three AU4G and three NX5. The day Motorail service between Euston and Edinburgh is formed of an NZ5, two AD1G, AJ1G, six AC2G, and two NX5 throughout plus five between Euston and Carlisle only. The Glasgow sleeper service is formed with six sleepers (AS4G/AU4G), AN1F, three sleepers, NH5 and four AC2Ds.

Polmadie Coaching Stock Depot, Glasgow, is responsible for maintaining six Mk3 sets for daytime Anglo–Scottish services. Booked formations are NZ5, two AD1G, AJ1G, six AC2G.

Longsight maintains four sets of Mk3 stock and eight sets of Mk2f stock for London services. The Mk3 sets are formed NZ5, three AD1H, AJ1G, five AD2G and the Mk2f sets are booked NZ5, two AD1F, AJ1G, six AD2F with an extra AD2F on three sets.

The complexities in variety of vehicle types and formations to maximise fleet availability leaves maintenance and operational staff with a major task to ensure that so far as possible on the day the correct formation is provided for each service, doubly essential when seat reservations have been sold. This route has for some time endeavoured to maintain specific coaches to each set to ensure reasonably even wear and tear and have true sets ready for scheduled maintenance and booked periodicity overhauls, not a 'rag-bag' of vehicles at different times as was the previous practice. A few spare vehicles are held as temporary replacements to be inserted when an unscheduled heavy repair is required, with the booked vehicle normally resuming its place at the earliest opportunity.

Most services on this route are booked for the fleet of 26 Class 87/0 and 15 Class 90/0 locomotives with 110mph maximum permitted speed. Sleeping car services are booked for a dedicated fleet of nine Class 87 locomotives restricted to 100mph. As these locomotives are relatively modern an 80% availability is diagrammed. The Birmingham route and occasional other services are diagrammed for haulage from a pool of three Class 86/1 and 22 Class 86/2 locomotives, booked for a 64% availability. The slight reduction in services with the winter timetable has not been reflected by any recorded changes to traction and rolling stock fleets.

Midland Lines

Administration for this route moved to Derby in April 1992 and was combined with Cross Country. As the rolling stock is effectively independent it is more easily understood separately.

A regular service of IC125 High Speed Trains is scheduled for the line, including two Pullman services each way. The London terminus is St Pancras and while some services call at Bedford, Wellingborough and/or Kettering the first main call is Leicester. Some then call at Loughborough, home of Brush Traction's Falcon Works where many diesel locomotives were constructed, and then the line divides with roughly alternate services routed via Nottingham or Derby to Sheffield. Both routes have a basic hourly service through the day supplemented by Regional Railways local and Express services north of Leicester. Twelve of the IC125 sets allocated to the route are identical to the East Coast sets and interchange has been frequent, although stricter control is intended and both the Class 43 power cars and the coaches are maintained at Neville Hill depot. Dedicated sets are allocated to two Pullman services; the Master Cutler (Derby & Sheffield) and the Robin Hood (Nottingham & Sheffield) which are formed Class 43, three GH1G, GK1G [TRFM Master Cutler, TRFB Robin Hood], three GH2G, GJ2G. Occasional services continue from Sheffield to Leeds to simplify movements to/from Neville Hill. Etches Park (Derby) and Bounds Green (London) depots also carry out overnight servicing and minor essential repairs.

Technically Wellingborough and Kettering come within the 80-mile radius of London, but traffic levels forecast do not warrant NSE extending its electrified service north of Bedford while complying with the Government financing requirements. The local DMU service became infrequent and unreliable and was discontinued in 1991. Development of a theme park at Corby failed to materialise and the shuttle to Kettering was discontinued after the local authority withdrew financial support. InterCity's peak period services are generally full without serving these two East Midlands commuter towns. Thus two services each way (up in the morning, down in the evening) are booked for Class 47/4 locomotive hauled Mk2f stock off Derby which serve these two towns plus Market Harborough, Leicester, Loughborough and Long Eaton. In the event of IC125 failure(s) the hauled set(s) may be called on to deputise; for this possibility and weekend cross-country duties a Mk1 Buffet Car is included in the basic Mk2f formation. Three sets are thus formed AD1E, AN21, two AC2F, AC2D, AE2F. The Class 47/4 locomotives are provided by the main InterCity fleet based at Bristol Bath Road. These two trains were to cease in a service revision next May, but a door lock safety modification programme to all IC125 stock has caused this to be deferred. An IC125 shuttle service is expected to be introduced between St Pancras and Leicester

Line speed throughout the route is a maximum of 110mph which allows single manning of the Class 43 power cars.

Cross Country

One look at the BR timetable, Table 51, shows the complexity of this service network. Although Derby is the administrative hub, Birmingham is the operating centre with London termini all but excluded.

The most widely used service title by this business is 'North East–South West' which well describes the Bristol–Birmingham–York corridor in the days of the 1970s & 1980s, but the area covered is much greater. As the Table head shows 'South Wales and South West–North West and North East England and Scotland via Birmingham' is certainly closer to fact.

Rolling stock comprises IC125 seven-coach sets and standard hauled stock of Mk2d to Mk2f designs. The locomotive fleet is Class 47/4 diesel and Class 86/2 electric traction.

The IC125 coaching sets are maintained at Edinburgh Craigentinny (11), St Philips Marsh (Bristol, 5) and Laira (Plymouth, 7). Each has one fewer First Class coach than the sets operated by the other InterCity businesses and are thus formed Class 43, GH1G, GK2G or GN1G, four GH2G, GJ2G, Class 43. Catering is limited to a hot and cold buffet rather than the full meal service provided on other IC125 routes.

A through service between Dundee and Penzance crosses the Forth Bridge to Edinburgh and proceeds down the East Coast main line to Doncaster with appropriate calls, thence via Sheffield, Derby, Birmingham New Street, the Lickey Incline, Bristol Temple Meads, Exeter and Plymouth in 11½ hours without a traction change or run round due to using an IC125. Another IC125 duty from Scotland is the 'Wessex Scot' along the East Coast route from Edinburgh to York, then via Leeds, Sheffield, Birmingham, continuing via Coventry, Oxford, Reading, Basingstoke and Southampton to Poole. Some services from Edinburgh take the West Coast route via Carstairs, Carlisle and Crewe to Birmingham New Street and Birmingham International with haulage by Class 86/2 electric locomotives. Most Cross Country locomotive hauled services have a converted Mk2f Restaurant First Lounge Car (AJ1F) offering similar service to the IC125 buffet. This coach is normally marshalled on the end of the train, thus the serving bar, available to all passengers, is on the 'inner' end divided by a swing door from the First Class lounge. The rest of the train comprises five AC2D/E or F coaches with either AE2D/E or F (allocated to Manchester sets from October 1992) or a Mk1 Gangwayed Brake van (currently on the Scottish based sets, but expected to be replaced). The seventh vehicle is also significant in permitting normal line speeds up to 100mph. Lower limits apply to shorter hauled trains for safe braking distances. Polmadie has a maintenance fleet of 15 such sets and Longsight has 14. The 'Devon Scot' (IC125) travels by the West Coast route between Edinburgh and Birmingham, thence to Plymouth, while the 'Sussex Scot' is hauled by a Class 86/2 from Edinburgh–Birmingham New Street, then forward with a Class 47/4 to Brighton (Eastbourne on summer Saturdays) via Kensington Olympia.

The final InterCity service of the day from Edinburgh is the sleeper, having trundled across from Glasgow Central via Motherwell. At Edinburgh three NX5 Motorail vehicles for Bristol are attached. The sleeper service then continues to Plymouth. The two sets are each formed of six AU4G, sleeper with pantry, coaches, and, new for 1992, an AG1E – an AD1E converted to provided a mini-buffet trolley point, plus a brake vehicle. No other seating accommodation is provided.

A day service from Edinburgh via Glasgow Central takes an IC125 set to Poole, via the West Coast route to Birmingham, thence Reading and Basingstoke. A quick interior clean precedes the train's return north to Manchester. A through service from Glasgow to Penzance, the 'Cornish Scot', via Birmingham and Bristol is also an IC125 set. Glasgow Central–Manchester Piccadilly–Stockport–Birmingham and Glasgow–Liverpool Lime Street locomotive hauled services are booked for Class 86/2 electric traction north of Preston and Class 47/4 diesel locomotives south thereof. Most Cross Country services from Liverpool and Manchester via Birmingham and Reading to Paddington ceased last March with extra services taking the Southampton route, others reversing at Reading. The Reading terminating and Paddington services are Class 47/4 locomotive hauled, south of Birmingham.

Other Cross Country IC125 services are Manchester Piccadilly–Bournemouth ('The Pines Express'), Leeds–Paignton ('The Devonian'), Leeds–Plymouth ('The Armada'), Leeds–Swansea, Newcastle and York–Birmingham New Street, thence to either Bristol Temple Meads or London Paddington; also Plymouth to Liverpool Lime Street or York.

One group of locomotive-hauled services is allocated coaching stock sets which are maintained at Derby Etches Park. A Liverpool–Dover Western Docks via Crewe, Birmingham, Reading, Kensington Olympia and Canterbury East, again changing between electric and diesel traction at Birmingham New Street, uses one of the five coaching sets formed AD1F, AG2D, four AC2F, AE2F. During route modernisation for the Channel Tunnel between October 1992 and May 1993 the Saturday service terminates at Canterbury East with local arrangements for Dover customers. The same train is booked back promptly to Liverpool, precluding alternative routeing. The future of this service is in doubt, even before the new Eurostar (Channel Tunnel) services commence. These coaching sets also form a York–Poole train via Sheffield, Derby, Birmingham and Reading and York–Swansea via Birmingham New Street and Cardiff. All these services operate with Class 47/4 diesel haulage throughout. A Manchester Piccadilly–Brighton service via Birmingham New Street (traction change) and Kensington Olympia is also diagrammed for Derby-based coaches. Other cross country services to South Wales are operated under the Regional Railways Express network.

A summer Saturday InterCity Holidaymaker service runs between Rose Grove (Lancashire) and Paignton via Blackburn, Preston, Birmingham New Street, Bristol, Exeter and Newton Abbot. This is booked for an InterCity Mk1 Charter set from the Liverpool Edge Hill fleet with Class 47/4 haulage.

Great Western

After the complexities of the Birmingham-centred Cross Country business the Great Western is more straightforward with just three main routes from Paddington. The administrative base is at Swindon, another of the past great railway towns, now the home of many City of London workers, and with its own scientific industry as well as motor construction for the Rover Group.

Operationally the benefit of 37 standard eight-coach formation IC225 sets (as East Coast but eight sets have an GN1G instead of GK1G Restaurant Car) allows ease of interchange between services. All scheduled day services are booked for these trains. Paddington is unable to handle many regular locomotive hauled services from mid-summer 1992 while major alterations are effected to the approaches and station signalling for ATP (Advanced Train Protection). Special arrangements will apply for sleeper and parcels trains and a facility using Platform 1A will be available for a very limited number of extra services. 'Top and tail' operations (locomotive at each end) are likely at least for the limited number of empty hauled stock movements between Old Oak Common and Paddington.

A standard pattern of departures and calling points provides best capacity over the route, remembering that NSE also has Express services, as far as Didcot and Bedwyn, with a 90mph speed limit on stock. InterCity also has to fit in some locomotive-hauled Cross Country services between Acton, Reading and Didcot. These lower speed trains, if delayed, can cause significant difficulties to IC125 services with peak period platform capacity at Paddington and Reading at a premium. InterCity services to Bristol Temple Meads and Weston-super-Mare, Bristol Parkway, Cardiff and Swansea, also Plymouth and Penzance, are all booked for the 125mph trains. One daily IC125 service from Paddington works to Milford Haven.

At holiday times a through service operates to Fishguard Harbour for sailings to Rosslare. For night sailings it is necessary to change at Swansea.

The only other scheduled InterCity service is the Paddington–Penzance sleeper. It stops to pick up at Reading, then at Exeter, before waiting over an hour at Plymouth, while part of the train is detached. It then calls at main points west. The 'up' service is just 15min at Plymouth attaching. These services are booked for four AU4G (sleeper with pantry) maintained at Plymouth Laira. Nightrider seating accommodation is provided in two coaches, a newly converted AG1F and AD2D maintained at Old Oak Common.

Anglia and Gatwick
InterCity places these two routes under a joint business operation although they have little in common. Perhaps the push-pull operation now enjoyed on both routes and the fact that neither track is actually under the Sector's responsibility places them in this unique situation.

In Anglia, InterCity operates a frequent service between Liverpool Street and Norwich and a boat train service to Harwich Parkeston Quay. Trains are booked for Class 86/2 locomotive power and formed two AD1F, AJ1G (six sets) or AJ41, two AC2F (64 seats), two AC2F (74 seats), AF2F. All stock is maintained at Norwich Crown Point depot. On summer Saturdays three Liverpool Street–Norwich services are extended to Great Yarmouth. For the extra $18\frac{1}{2}$ miles, non-electrified, a Class 47/4 diesel locomotive is hired from Rail express systems, the Class 86 electric locomotive remains attached to avoid technical problems. The Mk3 Restaurant Cars (AJ1G) were introduced in May 1992 for the East Anglian and other prime London–Norwich services. All other stock is Mk2f with little likelihood of further change for a few years. Boat train sets have an additional Mk1 Gangwayed Brake vehicle. Anglia now uses the 13 Driving Brake Standard Open vehicles (AF2F) previously owned by ScotRail, the only such main line stock on BR. As speeds do not exceed 100mph, passengers are allowed to travel in this vehicle, even when it is leading the train.

Gatwick Express services use passenger stock of Mk2f design built in 1973 and converted into fixed units in 1984 for operation with a Mk1 Driving Motor Luggage Van and Class 73/2 electro-diesel locomotives, normally operating only on the 750v dc electric supply system. Ten two-car and 18 three-car units were all refurbished at BREL Derby during 1991/92. Operation is usually in eight-car formations with services at 15min intervals for all but four hours at night. The service operates non-stop between Victoria and Gatwick Airport taking just

30min. NSE operates a slower, intermediate stop service with intermediate stops around the clock.

Charter

This business generally operates all long distance hired trains either with its own rolling stock or an approved fleet of privately owned vehicles. Services are not shown in the public timetable but a series of regular Leisure Cruises are planned and advertised well in advance. Relief InterCity services at Bank Holiday periods are not part of the Charter business although its standard stock may be utilised. It does not at present have its own dedicated locomotive fleet although eight Class 47/4s and one West Coast Class 86/2 are owned by InterCity for Charter use and the business also currently has the weekend use of four Railfreight Distribution Class 90/0 locomotives.

Charter aims to provide the service required by its customers. This can vary from using the restored Pullman coaches owned by Venice Simplon Orient Express (VSOE - Sea Containers Ltd) from London Victoria to Liverpool for the Grand National, to Mk1 Standard Open coaches, retired from front line service, but maintained to the best standards for football specials or steam hauled enthusiast trips. The only occasions on which InterCity is not involved with hired trains is if NSE or Regional Railways wish to operate a service within the confines of their area using their own resources.

VIP fleet:

Most of this fleet is based at Bounds Green, maintained alongside the latest Mk4 stock. Formations vary according to requirements and thus we summarise the available stock. The reduction in demand for sleeper services enabled Charter to take some surplus vehicles for VIP Land Cruises between London and the tourist areas of Scotland. A full at-seat dining service is offered to the hirer at appropriate times. For daytime travel a fleet of 11 Mk1 Kitchen coaches (types AJ11, AJ41 and AK51), 25 Mk1 First Open (AD11) and one Mk2d First Open (AD1D) are usually available. Other coaches in the fleet comprise an AA11, two AB11, five AB31 to provide conductor guard and brake van accommodation, and three AA1D. The business is beginning to take over some surplus Mk2d and Mk2e coaches to provide air conditioned comfort in the seated accommodation but, with the main businesses still requiring a few Mk1 Restaurant Cars and no Mk2 series built, catering will continue to be from 1960s stock. Fourteen Mk3 sleeping cars are maintained for these VIP services. Two AU51 coaches are provided for train staff employed on the Land Cruise sleeper services and are not for public use.

Summer Land Cruise trains to the North of Scotland are generally extensively cleaned during the layover at Inverness. A fleet of Mk1 coaches is then provided to take customers to Kyle of Lochalsh or Thurso/Wick. A few VIP vehicles are maintained at Old Oak Common Coaching Stock depot, west London. They comprise three AJ41, 11 AD1E and two AB1D used for specials such as Newbury and Cheltenham horse-race meetings. At the time of going to press it was expected that InterCity will maintain this stock elsewhere from summer 1993.

Steam fleet:

For the summer of 1992 InterCity only sponsored steam specials on the Fort William-Mallaig line in the West Highlands of Scotland. Nine AC21 and one each AB21 and AB31 were allocated to Bounds Green although they rarely ventured south of Fort William during the summer season. Some of the stock was withdrawn at the end of the season; a few vehicles were allocated to general charter use. Alternative stock which could be considered for summer 1993 was stored awaiting a decision.

General fleet:
A few general Charter fleet coaches are based at Bounds Green and available as emergency cover for the Mk4 fleet or for hire on an 'ordinary' charter with or without catering. The fleet comprises two AB1D, three AD1E, eight AC2D, two AC2E and two AJ41, to which a pair of sleepers were recently added.

Edge Hill CSD (Liverpool) has three sets each formed from five AC21 and an AB1D. Apart from a summer Saturday duty between Rose Grove and Paignton (see Cross Country) these are for hire as required. It also has a further ten AC21 and four AB1D for extra sets or strengthening. An air-conditioned charter set can be formed from two AD1E, two AC2D, eight AC2E and an AB1D vehicles. The fleet includes vehicles which operated from Inverness during the summer period.

Carlisle Upperby depot has a team of staff engaged on refurbishing interiors to the specialist requirements of the Charter fleet. Providing bodywork is sound the interior can be stripped and seating renovated; carpets, curtains, decor, lighting and tables renewed or restored. In many of the VIP fleet coaches table lamps have been fitted.

For the winter timetable Carlisle has again received a small fleet allocated for normal maintenance. Five AD1D, eight AD1E, two AB1D and two AN21 are available for charter.

Private owner:
All privately owned coaches to operate over BR lines have to be certificated for overall condition and carry a yellow oval plate, normally on the sole bar, indicating a BR identity number. A series of such numbers are allocated to each owner and these do not match the painted bodyside number which is usually its last running number in BR or pre-grouping company stock. This includes support coaches for preserved steam locomotives, used to convey and provide dormitory accommodation for owners touring with their pride.

To do justice to the efforts of enthusiasts who have contributed money and hard effort to the painstaking restoration of engines and coaches in main line running condition would require a book on its own. As the public passenger-carrying coaching sets can often be seen hauled by modern traction, brief details follow:

Glasgow & South Western Railway Co
Grandeur par excellence, this train may seem out of place in a review of today's BR rolling stock, but is nevertheless relevant in this context. To travel on this train costs a princely sum, but it is highly exclusive and aimed primarily at the American tourist wishing to survey Scotland's scenery and be treated like a Laird or Lady throughout the tour – a 'castle on wheels'. The train comprises an 1892 Caledonian Railway Observation Saloon, seating just 21, a London and North Western Railway Dining Saloon, a Great Northern Railway Family Saloon and five early BR Mk1 coaches including two Sleeper Firsts and a Brake Corridor coach. Haulage has to be mainly by a Class 37/4 locomotive except between Fort William and Mallaig where steam allows travellers to go into a 'time warp'.

During the season the train is maintained at Edinburgh Craigentinny depot and in the winter will normally be found at the Steamtown preservation centre, Carnforth, Lancashire.

Venice-Simplon Orient Express
A rake of original Pullman Car Co coaches built between 1928 and 1952, formerly used on services such as the Golden Arrow, Brighton Belle and Queen of Scots. The passenger carrying cars were usually named and the tradition is maintained with any numbers discreetly placed. Names now carried are *Audrey,*

Cygnus, Ibis, Lucille, Minerva, Perseus, Phoenix and *Zena*. Seating is all now officially First Class – luxury would be a more precise understatement! – and some non-passenger carrying vehicles are included. Seating varies from 20 to 48 per coach with accommodation varying from open-plan to a mini state-room. The train is owned by Sea Containers Ltd who maintain it at InterCity's Battersea Stewarts Lane Depot, London. Coaches are all painted in the Pullman umber and cream colours.

In 1991 Brighton recorded 150 years of railways to the town and for special celebrations organised by NSE locomotive No.73101 named *Brighton Evening Argus* (renamed in 1992 *The Royal Alex* after a Brighton hospital for the duration of a children's charity appeal) was similarly repainted including the Pullman branding and the former company's crests and worked with the train on some special trips. Sadly the locomotive is only suitable for such work on third rail dc lines (former Southern Region) as it is an unmodified version of the Gatwick Express locomotives. While normally now confined to hauling civil engineers trains it retains the Pullman colours and may occasionally appear with the VSOE train if so hired. The coaches have had air brakes and electric train heating fitted so that they are able to operate over most BR lines and a regular programme of tours is arranged during the summer including, as the name implies, operating to/from Folkestone for the Calais sea crossing to connect with the true VSOE.

The Manchester Pullman

This train was the forerunner of BR's Mk2 series coaches. Along with sister vehicles now scrapped it was the last of the true all First Class Pullman style coaches built for British Railways – today's Mk3b and Mk4 coaches are little different to ordinary First Class but provide the opportunity to charge higher catering prices to semi-captive hungry customers.

However as Mk3 coaches became available for the Euston–Manchester route InterCity determined that the fleet was surplus to normal requirements. All included asbestos insulation when built, the dangers at that time not having been identified. Luckily ten had this removed during overhaul and the Charter business Director considered them suitable. They were given an interior refurbishment at Carlisle Upperby, repainted and named appropriately to form a 'Lakeland Pullman'. The kitchen cars were named *Ullswater* and *Windermere*. Their new life was relatively short and they were withdrawn from BR stock. However a new company, Manchester Executive Travel, was formed to purchase and run the train in 1991. The two Pullman First with Kitchen cars are now named *The White Rose* and *The Red Rose*, seven Pullman Parlour First are *City of Manchester, Elizabethan, Prince Rupert, Golden Arrow, Caledonian, Southern Belle* and *King Arthur* with the Pullman Brake First *Talisman*.

Steam Locomotive Operators Association

A variety of 18 First Class Mk1 coaches is now owned by this organisation and painted in original crimson livery. Maintenance is contracted to Bounds Green depot, London. These are now dual braked to enable haulage by steam, diesel and electric traction. Steam haulage where train heating is necessary now requires the hire from InterCity of AB21 No.35469 which has a generator in the former brake van area. AJ41 No.1680 is similarly painted, although this restaurant car is officially still part of InterCity's fleet.

Traintours

This Manchester-based organisation has 12 Standard Class Mk1 coaches painted in the green livery of Pilkington Glass Co, St Helens. The stock is maintained at Edge Hill, Liverpool, and mainly used on charter duties originating in North West England.

King's Cross to Leeds was the inaugural route for Class 91 locomotives, initially with IC125 stock and now with Mk4 coaches. Class 91 No.91001 heads a London service into Leeds. *Brian Morrison*

Mk4 DVT No.82208 heads up the East Coast main line past Shipton-under-Beningborough, with a Newcastle–King's Cross service. Class 91 No.91008 provides power from the rear on 15th May 1992. Note the 'Edinburgh 200 miles' sign at the lineside. *Barry Nicolle*

An InterCity 125 set works a King's Cross–Aberdeen service north of York. The front end livery of Class 43 No.43067 was experimental. The buffers were fitted to just seven during special trials with Class 91s being controlled from the Class 43 acting as a Driving Van Trailer. *Barry Nicolle*

The 12.18 Bournemouth–Newcastle IC125 Cross Country service seen passing Southampton in May 1992. The Mk3 coaches are much more comfortable than their predecessors. The IC125s are limited to 110mph throughout most Cross Country journeys as very little of the route is passed for higher speeds. *Brian Morrison*

A summer dated relief Cross Country service at York for Exeter via Leeds, Sheffield, Derby, Birmingham and Bristol, awaits departure time on 14th May 1992, hauled by Class 47/4 No.47812. *Barry Nicolle*

A fleet of 14 eight-coach IC125s work the Midland main line between St Pancras and Sheffield via Derby or Nottingham. A southbound service is seen awaiting departure from Sheffield led by Class 43 No.43198 with 'sister' No.43061 at the rear together providing 4,500hp. This is almost twice the power of standard diesel locomotive hauled services on the route. *Brian Morrison*

Two locomotive hauled train sets form peak period services between Derby and St Pancras; the 17.30 is seen leaving the London terminus on 21st July 1992 headed by Class 47/4 No.47839. *Brian Morrison*

Class 90 No.90004 heads a West Coast route Glasgow Central express service from Euston. The first 15 of the class of 50 were built by BREL Crewe Works for this InterCity route and after a chequered start they are now amongst the most reliable of BR's locomotive fleet. *Brian Morrison*

The Euston–Wolverhampton service is booked for Class 86/2 locomotives hauling Mk2f and Mk3 coaches. This is the next major route InterCity want to modernise when funding is available, whether through private or government investment. No.86251 is seen heading a northbound service at Cardington. *Brian Morrison*

Mk3 Driving Van Trailer (DVT) No.82129, seen at Wolverhampton, stands at the head of a London bound service whilst Royal Mail traffic is loaded. The Mk3 DVTs are used with either Mk2f or Mk3 standard coaches on West Coast services. They enable push-pull operation of all but sleeper services on this route and thus save on the number of locomotives required, also time and staff at termini. *Brian Morrison*

The southbound Night Aberdonian service is seen just outside Aberdeen on 27th May 1992 hauled by Class 37/0 locomotives 37251 and 37252. Motorail vans are behind the locomotives, with the Stagecoach Rail seating accommodation and InterCity sleepers included in the train. Electric traction takes over at Edinburgh Waverley. *Cyril Loftus*

The only non-sleeper customers on the Night Aberdonian are conveyed in two Mk2d Standard Open coaches. The coaches were leased exclusively by Stagecoach Rail, a road coach company providing connections at Edinburgh for Perth and Inverness. This private enterprise venture, complete with hostess service and light breakfast at a competitive price, was unable to sell sufficient seats for viability. InterCity revised the contract and resumed ticket sales, whilst allowing Stagecoach facilities to sell seats on the Glasgow sleepers. The coaches are seen between the sleepers and Motorail vans. *Brian Morrison*

Left The Night Aberdonian Sleeper and Motorail service is seen at Euston on 18th June 1992 waiting departure hauled by Class 87 No.87005. Sleeper services should always be hauled between Euston and Edinburgh by Class 87 locomotives; when Class 90s were used they were frequently 'borrowed' at Edinburgh for East Coast duties and not available for the booked return duty. *Brian Morrison*

Below left Locomotives are usually at the London end of the Liverpool Street–Norwich services, contrary to other routes using push-pull operation. No.86230 stands at the recently rebuilt London terminus on 19th February 1992. The front end cables are for the electrical circuitry for controlling the Time Division Multiplex equipment allowing push-pull working. *Brian Morrison*

Below Thirteen former ScotRail Mk2f Driving Brake Standard Open (DBSO) coaches are used for InterCity Anglia services to allow push-pull operation and save on locomotives and termini shunting staff. Unlike on the later built DVTs, customers are allowed to travel in these vehicles as speeds must not exceed 100mph. No.9709 is seen heading a Liverpool Street–Parkeston Quay Boat Train through Bethnal Green. *Brian Morrison*

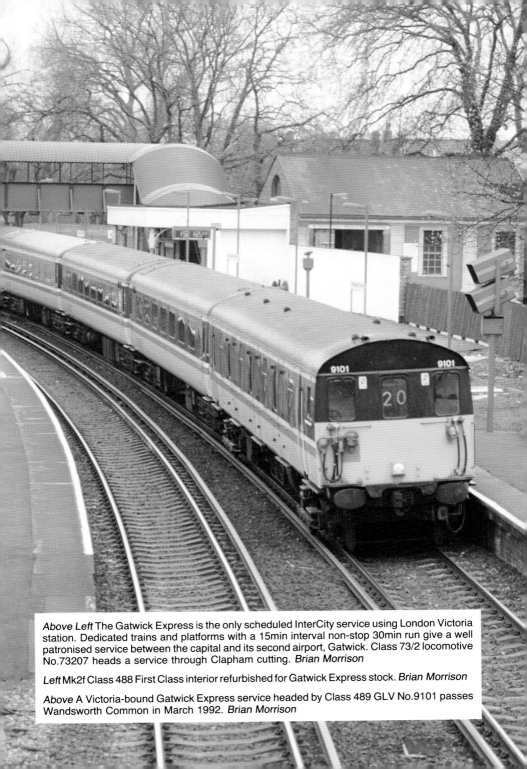

Above Left The Gatwick Express is the only scheduled InterCity service using London Victoria station. Dedicated trains and platforms with a 15min interval non-stop 30min run give a well patronised service between the capital and its second airport, Gatwick. Class 73/2 locomotive No.73207 heads a service through Clapham cutting. *Brian Morrison*

Left Mk2f Class 488 First Class interior refurbished for Gatwick Express stock. *Brian Morrison*

Above A Victoria-bound Gatwick Express service headed by Class 489 GLV No.9101 passes Wandsworth Common in March 1992. *Brian Morrison*

The VSOE Pullman stands at Brighton on 2nd May 1992 with appropriately Pullman liveried Class 73/1 No.73101, newly named *The Royal Alex* (after a Brighton hospital). *Brian Morrison*

VSOE Pullman interior view. *Brian Morrison*

Mk3 sleeping cars repainted in the InterCity business colours, including white roofs, for the VIP Charter fleet. *Brian Morrison*

Mk4 First Class interior. *Brian Morrison*

A Chester–Birmingham express service passes Rhosymedre on 26th June 1992 formed by Central Division, Norwich based, Class 158 No.158783. These units have a wide area of operation and work from East Anglia to Birmingham and then a few duties to Shrewsbury, Aberystwyth and Chester. *Brian Morrison*

REGIONAL RAILWAYS

This business is the most complex as it involves almost all lines outside the Network SouthEast area and occasional overlaps as will be indicated. Whilst InterCity operates the long distance trains, usually centred on London or Birmingham, Regional Railways also has some long through cross-country journeys such as Glasgow–Sunderland, Newcastle–Liverpool, Harwich–Liverpool and Milford Haven–Portsmouth. The advantage of modern DMUs is that much less maintenance is required and fuel capacity allows 850 miles from a Pacer unit, 1,200 miles from a Class 150 Sprinter and 1,500 miles or more from Classes 155-158. Relatively large fleets spread amongst the five Divisions help with driver and conductor knowledge, allowing for a very quick crew change at strategic en-route locations.

Regional Railways has thus three major roles. Provision of a commuter service around the cities and large towns to all urban conurbations outside the south east of England, secondly to provide a regular, reasonably fast, economic cross-country service where numbers of customers do not warrant the traditional seven-plus locomotive hauled coaches of an InterCity train and including the best possible connections to/from the trunk route services. For example InterCity has deemed uneconomic services to Shrewsbury, Blackpool and, from May, Grimsby and Cleethorpes. Regional Railways' aim is to see that the inconvenience of changing at Wolverhampton or Birmingham, Preston and Newark respectively is minimised and that the overall journey time does not suffer. InterCity's London–Holyhead service was cut by 50% to just three per day but Regional Railways provides a regular service with its best trains connecting with InterCity West Coast and Cross Country services at Crewe. Finally, Regional Railways provides a low cost community service in rural areas with single- or two-coach units.

Diagramming of rolling stock is very complex as it is imperative to obtain maximum benefits whilst allowing appropriate time for cleaning, washing, servicing and maintenance. Availability requirements for peak periods vary from around 70% for first generation stock, to 80% on Pacers to nearly 90% on Sprinters and Express units. At the shoulders of the day or at peak periods or Sundays many variations from the standard pattern may be diagrammed. In the following brief summary only some services operate over the full distance shown, for example between Newcastle and Liverpool stations at York, Leeds, Manchester (Oxford Road, Piccadilly or Victoria) are typical points for starting or terminating in accordance with the timetable.

Express Services

This operation is the most important flagship service for Regional Railways. It covers a wide range of long distance routes not covered by InterCity. The 1988 introduction of a regular service using 75mph Classes 155 and 156 Super Sprinters on significant long distance routes was popular with the public and led to appreciable traffic growth. Over the last two years they have gradually been replaced by the 90mph Class 158 of lightweight aluminium body construction – the first on BR – and designed with an enhanced interior specification including air-conditioning, public telephone and special facilities, including a toilet for the disabled. Many of the trains provide connections in and out of long distance InterCity services, showing that BR is still a single company with co-ordinating businesses.

Economy is achieved by having all vehicles powered by a small diesel mechanical engine and, while almost all have driving cabs, between two and 12 vehicles can operate in multiple depending on normal traffic demand, platform lengths and passing facilities on single lines. In practice no duties, other than short distance empty stock movements to/from servicing/maintenance depots, are booked for more than six vehicles

The rolling stock is allocated to four of the five Regional Railways area businesses but is mainly employed on cross-boundary duties to all five areas plus NSE!

ScotRail's Haymarket depot, Edinburgh, maintains 46 two-car sets to operate between Glasgow Queen Street and Edinburgh Waverley via Falkirk High; Glasgow and Edinburgh to Perth, Inverness, Dundee and Aberdeen. Some Inverness–Elgin–Aberdeen, Glasgow Queen St–Cumbernauld and via Falkirk Grahamston to Dunblane services are also diagrammed for these units on 'filling in' duties.

Inverness depot carries out some servicing and Perth the overnight heavy cleaning. Regional Railways has found the demand on its main Edinburgh services to warrant First Class seating areas, although only 31 sets so far have this and the other 15 sets are due for the modification by early 1993. This reversed a national policy decision to run all Regional Railways trains as Standard Class only.

The **North East** has two depots maintaining the Express service trains. Heaton, Newcastle, is responsible for the 17 North Trans-Pennine three-car and ten two-car sets that mainly ply between Newcastle–York–Leeds–Manchester Piccadilly–Liverpool Lime Street and a few services which are routed between Darlington and York via Middlesbrough. Some services are routed between York, Scarborough and Filey instead of further north. Contrary to original plans these are the only three-car RR Express sets. The three-car units also have occasional duties from Liverpool to Holyhead, Liverpool to Wigan North Western, Rochdale–Manchester Victoria–Liverpool Lime Street, Selby–Bradford Interchange–Manchester Victoria and on Sundays between Leeds and Hull. The two-car sets also have Sunday duties from Micklefield to Rochdale and a Scarborough–York service.

The section of Neville Hill depot, Leeds, sponsored by Regional Railways maintains three fleets of Express units as well as stock for other long distance and local services. Ten units, Class 158/9 are specially painted crimson and cream as they are leased by BR to the West Yorkshire PTE (Metro). They mainly operate Newcastle–York–Leeds–Bradford Interchange – Halifax – Manchester Victoria–St Helens–Liverpool. Occasional booked duties see them working between Micklefield and Rochdale, Manchester Oxford Road and Chester, and York–Selby–Doncaster.

Regional Railways North-East also base 23 Class 158/0 units at Neville Hill for Leeds–Sheffield, Manchester or Crewe–Chester–Holyhead, Liverpool Lime Street–Manchester Piccadilly–Newcastle or Middlesbrough, Manchester Piccadilly–Cleethorpes, Hull or Nottingham, York–Halifax or Rochdale. A Saturday duty employs a unit on the Manchester Piccadilly–Blackpool North service.

Central base a fleet of 39 units at Norwich Crown Point and they cover an extremely wide area, of which the Norfolk town is far from central geographically. Apart from the daily boat train to Harwich Parkeston Quay, for the Hook of Holland ferry, and occasional duties to Ipswich, Express originate services at Norwich and at Stansted Airport (until May 1993 when they will use Cambridge as the terminus) with the two routes combining for the Ely–Peterborough section. At Peterborough, a major interchange point, Regional Railways routes divide; west to Leicester and Birmingham or north via Loughborough, Nottingham, Sheffield, Manchester Piccadilly and Warrington to Liverpool. A few services are routed over the East Coast main line between Peterborough and Grantham, then to Nottingham, while some travel from Nottingham to Derby, instead of Alfreton and Mansfield, en route to Sheffield. With cyclic diagramming some units regularly form the fast service between Birmingham–Shrewsbury–Chester or Aberystwyth. Some Norwich services are extended to Great Yarmouth and Lowestoft. Through services between Nottingham–Birmingham New Street–Worcester–Gloucester–Cardiff and also some on the Nottingham–Derby–Crewe line are diagrammed for this fleet.

The **South Wales and West** group of Express services has Cardiff as a base and maintains the stock at a refitted carriage depot at Cardiff Canton, adjacent to Trainload Freight's locomotive depot. A fleet of 37 units is currently maintained here, including the ten higher powered units, Nos. 158863-72. More of these 400hp units were ordered but requirements altered and the contract was taken over by Network SouthEast for their West of England line. Canton's diagrams do not differentiate duties for the 400hp engined vehicles. While most services commence at Cardiff to run east, a few also run west to Swansea, Llanelli, Carmarthen, Haverfordwest and Milford Haven. East from Cardiff all services run to Newport, then either via the Severn Tunnel to Bristol Parkway and/or Temple Meads or north to Crewe via Hereford and Shrewsbury, thence mainly to Manchester, although one Cardiff–Holyhead service connects with the Dun Laoghaire night ferry and one is routed to Liverpool Lime Street. Bristol Temple Meads forms a junction south east or south west. The westerly service runs to Exeter, then either Paignton or Plymouth and Penzance. The majority of Express services via Bristol travel hourly via Westbury, Salisbury and Southampton to Portsmouth Harbour. A few services are booked for four-cars between Cardiff and Fareham where the two sets divide, one for Chichester, Worthing and Brighton, the other to Portsmouth. Problems with clearances at Shoreham precluded Class 158s from working to Brighton prior to May 1992 and Class 155s were allocated to the service. Bristol Temple Meads–Weymouth and Swindon–Exeter–Paignton or Penzance are occasional duties booked for the Canton 158 fleet.

A lot of previously well documented early problems beset introduction of Class 158s. Although the major problems have been remedied a programme of further modifications must continue at ABB Transportation's (BREL) Derby Carriage Works for the immediate future. This has been allowed for in the diagrammed availability for the fleet, which shows that there will be room for a few extra services by these trains. ScotRail had planned to introduce a 15min interval service on the Edinburgh–Falkirk High–Glasgow route throughout the main part of the day, but capacity problems from proposed expansion of other Strathclyde services to Glasgow Queen Street and the alternative InterCity service to Glasgow Central leaves this plan on the shelf.

ScotRail

The main Regional Railways services in Scotland are the Express services referred to in the last section. There are of course many more local services, which, with a few exceptions, are all formed of modern or fully refurbished multiple unit stock.

Inverness has seven Class 156 Sprinter DMUs for the services to Wick, Thurso, Kyle of Lochalsh, Huntly, Dyce, and Aberdeen and a service from Montrose to Aberdeen. Until modifications to the Class 158 fleet are completed one diagram, two services each way over the winter period between Inverness and Aberdeen, has caused the retention of Class 37/4 locomotives and coaches on this self-contained service. A second locomotive hauled train may be required during the summer period. The summer Hebridean Heritage train runs between

Inverness and Kyle formed of retrimmed early Mk2 coaches repainted into Highland green, also a former DMU trailer car refitted to make an Observation Saloon, hauled by a Class 37/0 locomotive. Westbound the saloon is at the rear of the train, but eastbound it is immediately behind the locomotive. A similar train without saloon ran through the peak summer period of 1992, at other times the service is formed of a Sprinter. Consideration is being given to providing a second Observation Saloon service.

Corkerhill depot in west Glasgow maintains three fleets of Class 156 Sprinters. The Glasgow and South Western (GSW) line, Strathclyde Passenger Transport Executive (SPTE) and the West Highland (WH) line fleets of seven, 13 and eight respectively each have their own characteristics. Most of the SPTE sponsored fleet is painted in orange livery, all others are painted in the original two-tone Provincial blue, while the WH fleet has to have Radio Electronic Token Block signalling equipment. Although each group is separately diagrammed borrowing is common, including using Haymarket allocated stock, to cover any temporary shortages.

The Glasgow Central–Kilmarnock–Carlisle–Newcastle–Sunderland route forms the main duties for the GSW fleet. The Glasgow Central–Stranraer and Glasgow Central–East Kilbride duties are shared with the SPTE sets. The SPTE units also work to Barrhead, Kilmarnock and Livingstone South. The WH fleet mainly forms services between Glasgow Queen Street and Oban, Fort William and Mallaig. In the peak summer seasons of 1990 and 1992 three extra sets have been made available which when divided enables three-car units to be formed. A locomotive hauled train was also provided for the Glasgow–Fort William service during the summer of 1992 with extra luggage van accommodation for cyclists and campers. Filling in duties for this fleet are between Glasgow Queen Street and Cumbernauld, Dunblane, Stirling and Falkirk Grahamston.

Corkerhill is to grow in importance; it is having to add some 30-year old Class 101 units to its maintenance fleet to cover for additional services sponsored by Strathclyde PTE. Initially it has three newly refurbished units to cover the two diagram expanded service on the Glasgow Central–Paisley Canal line. From next May SPTE requirements will need seven additional units. SPTE are proposing to purchase 25 new Class 157 units, probably similar to either Class 156 or Class 165, to eliminate the old units and expand rail services around Glasgow.

Glasgow Shields depot is the only electric traction maintenance depot in Scotland. Whilst it provides emergency repair facilities for electric locomotives it is responsible for all electric multiple units working in Scotland. South Clyde services are formed of Class 303 units centred on Glasgow Central (High Level). Services round the Cathcart Circle, to Newton, Neilston, Wemyss Bay and Gourock are formed of single units off-peak or two units at peak periods. Services to Ayr, Largs and Ardrossan are formed of the Class 318 fleet.

Ironically North Clyde services now also work through Glasgow Central Low Level to the south east of the city. The southerly point is Lanark from where Class 303 units form a service via Glasgow Central LL to Milngavie. From Coatbridge Central services run via Motherwell and Hamilton via Glasgow Central LL to Singer and Dalmuir formed of Class 314 stock. The newest units, Class 320, operate the Helensburgh Central–Yoker–Airdrie–Drumgelloch service. The Balloch–Airdrie service is formed of Class 303 units and the Springburn–Milngavie by Class 314 units. Variations to stock provided, especially substitution by Class 303 units, occurs according to daily availability.

The recently electrified line to North Berwick has a regular service via Edinburgh Waverley to Haymarket. This line is the only duty in ScotRail for four-car Class 305 EMUs, which normally travel empty between Edinburgh and

Glasgow Shields depot for maintenance.

The Glasgow Underground is independently operated by Strathclyde Transport and has no direct connection with British Rail.

Haymarket Sprinter Depot, Edinburgh, is currently the home for seven three-car, first generation DMUs. These are able to act as substitutes for Class 150 Sprinters, which of course can in turn deputise for Classes 156 or 158, but their six diagrammed duties daily are on peak period Fife Circle (Edinburgh–Dunfermline–Cowdenbeath–Glenrothes–Kirkcaldy–Edinburgh), also Cardenden, Dunblane and Perth services. The three-car Class 101, some newly overhauled and painted in Regional Railways colours, are slower than the two-car Class 150 but have greater capacity. ScotRail is unable at this time to obtain additional Class 150 units, but it is planned to replace these with seven three-car Class 117 units from Central in May 1993.

The Fife Circle is served throughout the day by Class 150 Sprinters. A new station opened last summer is Glenrothes with Thornton, to encourage customers to the well known golf course to join local residents travelling by train. Other services from Edinburgh Waverley to Bathgate, Stirling, Perth and Dundee keep the modest fleet of 16 Class 150s very active.

The two main services between Glasgow and Edinburgh have already been mentioned in this book. The third is routed via Livingstone South and West Calder as a service for local residents to travel to and from either city. One evening duty has a unit working from Edinburgh to West Calder and then diverging to Motherwell. These are amongst duties for Haymarket's fleet of 11 Class 156 units. The other booked duties from Edinburgh are to Bathgate and Dunblane, also between Glasgow Queen Street and Cumbernauld, Falkirk Grahamston and Dunblane.

North East

As already indicated this area is dual-centred on the cities of Newcastle and Leeds with maintenance depots at Heaton and Neville Hill respectively. The former depot shares maintenance facilities with Rail express systems (Parcels), the latter with InterCity. Overhead electrification is provided at part of Heaton (for servicing the IC225 stock) and at Neville Hill (for IC225 and Regional Railways EMUs).

Units for the North Trans-Pennine Express route between Newcastle and Liverpool is the main commitment for **Heaton** depot but a wide range of other duties in the area of Newcastle, Sunderland, Middlesbrough and Darlington are included. The Newcastle area has had many changes over the years to its its DMU fleet, and many travellers will doubtless welcome the recent reduction to 15 Pacer railbuses, others having been replaced by Class 153 single cars and two-car Class 156 units. Some Class 142s are being repainted into the Tyne & Wear yellow livery previously carried by some Class 143s. The Pacer fleet's duties are generally on local services between Gateshead Metro Centre–Sunderland–Seaham and Gateshead–Middlesbrough–Nunthorpe. Saltburn–Middlesbrough–Bishop Auckland, extended to Stanhope on summer Sundays, Hexham–Sunderland and Middlesbrough, Morpeth–Sunderland and Middlesbrough–Whitby are the other routes they operate.

Services from Newcastle to Berwick-upon-Tweed, Carlisle, Middlesbrough, and Sunderland are covered by Heaton's eight Class 156 units and some by through workings from ScotRail and North West businesses. The seven Class 153 vehicles have a similar area of operation to the Class 156, but also Bishop Auckland–Darlington–Middlesbrough, Redcar and Saltburn local services. Heaton has a small fleet of locomotive hauled coaches, not in scheduled service, usually provided for football excursions.

Neville Hill's allocation reflects the highly urban nature of traffic in the Leeds and Bradford areas whilst York, Scarborough, Hull, Doncaster and Grimsby require a mixture of units. Doncaster–Wakefield–Leeds is a prime InterCity route with some local patronage, and therefore West Yorkshire Passenger Transport Executive lease three new Class 321/9 EMUs normally to work the local services, also occasionally diagrammed for a Class 142 or 144 Pacer, which connects at both ends of the route with trains for many other areas.

The fleet of 33 Class 158 units has been covered in our Express review. A current fleet of 19 Class 156 units generally work services over all routes between Leeds and Sheffield from where they work via Doncaster and Goole to Hull, also the short journey to Barnsley. The scenic Settle and Carlisle line is booked for this fleet with services from Leeds to Carlisle and one through to Dumfries. Local services from Doncaster to Selby and Hull to Bridlington are also covered by Class 156 units.

The seven Class 155 units are sponsored by Metro, West Yorkshire PTE, mainly to form the Leeds–Bradford Interchange–Hebden Bridge–Preston services, occasionally extended to Barrow-in-Furness or Blackpool.

A fleet of 19 Class 141, 27 Class 142, 13 two-car and 10 three-car Class 144 Pacer units cover a wide range of local duties. The Class 142s also operate a few longer distance services, often in multiple with Classes 155 or 156, to provide additional capacity on a peak service or balancing move. The narrow-bodied Class 141 units operate the Leeds–York service via Harrogate or Selby, Leeds–Knottingley via Castleford or Wakefield Westgate, Doncaster–Goole and Scunthorpe, Wakefield Kirkgate to Sheffield and Knottingley, Leeds–Castleford–Sheffield, Huddersfield–Barnsley–Sheffield and York–Sheffield–Chesterfield. The Class 142 fleet is diagrammed from Leeds to Doncaster, Huddersfield, Ilkley, Knottingley, Marsden, Selby and York. Huddersfield to Manchester Victoria, Sheffield, Wakefield Kirkgate and Westgate; Hull to Beverley, Bridlington, Doncaster, Filey, Scarborough, York via Selby and the East Coast main line or Church Fenton; also Bradford Forster Square to Ilkley are the relatively short duties. The units provide extra capacity on some Leeds–Blackpool North services. The Class 144s have dedicated diagrams for the two- and three-car units although generally over the same routes. From Leeds they work to Bradford Forster Square and Interchange, Doncaster, Goole, Halifax, Harrogate, Horton-in-Ribblesdale, Ilkley, Knaresborough, Lancaster, Selby, Skipton, and from Bradford Forster Square to Keighley, Ilkley and Skipton. Two-car units additionally work a Leeds–Castleford–Knottingley–Wakefield Westgate service, also Leeds–Marsden, Hull and York plus Doncaster–Scunthorpe.

The line from Leeds to Bradford Forster Square, Skipton and Ilkley is being electrified and a fleet of 14 new Class 323 trains was proposed for the service from mid-1994, but leasing has proved a political stumbling block and some Class 305s may have to be saved from the scrapyard as a short term measure. The planned service would require about 21 old units due to the extra maintenance necessary and this can only be achieved by cutting services elsewhere or major overhaul including gangway fitting on some first series Class 305s or Class 304s!

North West

This business area extends from Carlisle to Crewe, and Blackpool and Liverpool to east of Manchester where it joins the North East business. It has six depots to maintain the rolling stock – Edge Hill, Liverpool, for hauled coaches, Newton Heath, Manchester for new generation DMUs, Longsight Diesel Depot, Manchester, for first generation DMUs and the adjacent Longsight Electric Depot currently maintaining the aged Classes 304 and 305 EMUs, but due to receive a fleet of new Class 323 EMUs in part replacement this summer. Merseyrail lines from Liverpool Central to Southport, Hunts Cross, Ormskirk and Kirkby third-rail EMUs are maintained at Hall Road and also serviced at Kirkdale. Wirral line units operate between Moorfields (central Liverpool) and New Brighton, West Kirby and Rock Ferry (Birkenhead) pending extending to Chester. These units are based at Birkenhead North depot which also carries out overhauls on all Merseyrail units.

Edge Hill Coaching Stock Depot has six sets of coaches with at least three in daily use, extra at weekends; as insufficient good condition DMUs are available to meet peak demand services. Regional Railways, to their credit, still believe that 30-year old first generation DMUs, even after mini-refurbishment, are not good enough for commuters from Southport and Blackpool to Manchester Victoria. Five sets are all similarly formed with an AE2A and four AC2A/B or C coaches recently repainted and restored to reasonable standards of interior. In addition to the commuter trains from Southport and Blackpool they also operate a Blackpool–Liverpool service hauled by a single Class 31/4. On Fridays a set on a morning duty from Blackpool to Liverpool is hauled empty with a Class 37/4 locomotive to Cardiff to work a 17.15hrs to Manchester as this cannot be worked into available Class 158 diagrams. On summer Saturdays a Warrington Bank Quay–Bangor–Manchester Victoria– Llandudno–Liverpool duty, also Manchester Victoria–Holyhead and Birmingham New Street–Pwllheli and return are formed from these sets. A sixth set comprises four AC21 and one AB2C mainly for summer Cambrian Coast duties or steam charters. A few additional coaches are available as spares.

For the first time in the 1992 summer **Newton Heath** received some Super Sprinters, the fleet now comprising 15 Class 156 and 13 Class 153 units. The latter single car units work from Carlisle on Cumbrian Coast duties to Whitehaven, Workington and Barrow-in-Furness, also local duties from Carlisle to Dumfries. Duties between Manchester Victoria and Barrow-in-Furness and also Chester bring them to and from their home depot for overnight maintenance or change over. North Wales services between Llandudno and Blaenau Ffestiniog also via Bangor to Holyhead and Wrexham General–Bidston and a Bangor–Chester–Crewe duty are now also diagrammed for these single cars.

The popular Class 156 units are diagrammed to operate Blackpool North–Preston–Bolton–Stockport or Manchester Victoria, Barrow in Furness–Manchester Oxford Road or Victoria, Barrow–Carlisle line, Dumfries–Carlisle–Newcastle–Sunderland, Preston–Morecambe–Heysham Sea Terminal, Manchester Victoria–Llandudno or Bangor, Oxenholme–Windermere and Stockport–Stalybridge.

The North West fleet of Class 150 units comprises six formed into three-car sets to operate selected duties between Buxton–Manchester Piccadilly–Blackpool North and Southport, Manchester Piccadilly–Sheffield and filling in duties between Manchester Victoria–Shaw and Crompton and Blackburn. The 22 two-car units also operate these routes and additionally Wigan Wallgate–Manchester Piccadilly–Chester, some duties to Marple or New Mills Central. One set is diagrammed from Manchester Piccadilly to Cardiff on Saturday evening, returning on Sunday. Services from Manchester Victoria–Wigan North Western–Liverpool Lime Street, also to Huddersfield and Wakefield; Liverpool Lime Street–St Helens Central, Preston and Barrow-in-Furness; Blackpool North–Colne and Wigan Wallgate–Kirkby are other diagrammed duties for two-car Class 150/1 and 150/2 units.

A current fleet of 53 Class 142 Pacers operate widely throughout the region. Services from Manchester Victoria for Blackburn, Leeds and Wakefield via Huddersfield, Liverpool Lime St, Rochdale (all routes), Wigan Wallgate and

Wrexham General via Chester are included. From Manchester Piccadilly stopping services to Sheffield via Belle Vue or Stockport, to Doncaster and Hull, also local duties to Marple, Rose Hill Marple, New Mills Central and Chinley are so diagrammed. The Manchester Piccadilly–Liverpool Lime Street via Warrington Central and occasional Hazel Grove–Blackpool North stopping services are also scheduled for Pacer units. Other duties from Liverpool Lime Street are to Wigan North Western and Blackpool North. Local services between Blackpool South–Preston–Colne, Lancaster–Morecambe–Heysham Sea Terminal, Preston–Ormskirk are similarly scheduled. Outside the area Newton Heath's Pacers have filling in duties between Sheffield–Huddersfield and York, York–Selby–Doncaster and York–Church Fenton–Hull.

Longsight Diesel depot, Manchester, has 15 diagrams for first generation units. Many of these have had an interior refurbishment since late 1991 which should allow $3\frac{1}{2}$ years use without further major expense, and by next May all units in use here should come into this category. The fleet comprises nine twin-power car, 600hp, units to operate between Manchester Victoria and Llandudno or Wrexham General via Chester and between Chester–Hooton–Helsby. An active fleet of 16 standard two-car, 300hp, units work from Manchester Piccadilly to Marple, Rose Hill Marple, Chinley and Hazel Grove and from Manchester Victoria to Llandudno and Todmorden. The 300hp units are also diagrammed to operate local night staff trains from Manchester Piccadilly to Ashburys, Guide Bridge, Mottram Yard and Stockport, also between Manchester Victoria and Newton Heath depot.

Longsight Electric depot based EMUs form services from Manchester Piccadilly to Wilmslow, Stoke-on-Trent, Stafford, Crewe, Hadfield and Glossop, also between Crewe and Liverpool. The existing Classes 304 and 305 will mostly be replaced during 1993 by new Class 323 units although some Class 305s will be retained for Hadfield line services.

The Manchester Victoria–Bury line service ceased to be operated by BR in the early autumn of 1991 and from March 1992 became a Light Railway operation with trams by Metrolink for the Greater Manchester PTE which subsequently extended into the city, also to Piccadilly and to Altrincham.

Central

From Pwllheli and Aberystwyth in the west to Great Yarmouth and Lowestoft in the east is a general guide to the large territory forming Regional Railways Central division. Its main headquarters are Birmingham, appropriately with a heavy maintenance depot at Tyseley, and an area administration for East Anglia at Norwich, including a maintenance depot shared with InterCity.

Details have already been given of the extensive Express service from East Anglia to the West Midlands and North West of England operated by Class 158 units from Crown Point, Norwich depot. As InterCity has ceased to run regular London services beyond Wolverhampton to Shrewsbury or Saturday duties to the Cambrian Coast, Regional Railways has taken over the commitment by adding this section to its Shrewsbury–Aberystwyth service including providing some Class 158 units. An added attraction at Aberystwyth is the narrow gauge Vale of Rheidol railway, now in private ownership, running through the scenic Rheidol Valley to Devil's Bridge. The Little Railways of Wales rely extensively on BR's local services, especially for the summer tourist season, thus during the week it is worth changing from the Class 158 at Machynlleth to the Class 150 Sprinter for the journey to Pwllheli, calling at Tywyn for the Talyllyn Railway or Minffordd for the Ffestiniog Railway – some services connect at Blaenau Ffestiniog with BR trains to Llandudno Junction to provide an interesting round trip. The popular Pwllheli holiday camp is served by Penychain station. A summer Saturday service between Birmingham and Pwllheli uses a six-coach hauled train set from Edge Hill, Liverpool, powered by two of the three dedicated Class 31/1 locomotives based at Bescot specially fitted with RETB equipment. At other times the locomotives are allocated to infrastructure duties on the route. Other services to Shrewsbury are from Chester (see North West), Cardiff (see Express) and West Wales (see South Wales and West).

Birmingham, already mentioned at the heart of InterCity Cross Country services, is with Wolverhampton in close proximity a major conurbation with many towns to be served by the railway. Local services are sponsored by Centro, the West Midlands PTE, whose bright lime green and yellow livery adorns many of the area's Sprinter DMUs and the new Class 323 EMUs between Lichfield Trent Valley, Sutton Coldfield and Birmingham New Street. From May 1993 these should continue south via Longbridge to Redditch. The newly electrified northern part of the CrossCity line was due to see Class 323s from 30th November, but delayed availability has caused a few life extinct Class 304s to receive attention at BRML Wolverton to allow a short extension in service. Some rearrangement of duties has seen a temporary interchange between Classes 304 and 310.

An existing electric multiple unit service formed from a fleet of 11 'Midline' (previous marketing title for WMPTE services) liveried Class 310/1 four-car units operate between Walsall–Birmingham New Street–Coventry, and a few local services between Stafford–Birmingham–Coventry. The units are serviced at a small depot, Soho, just west of New Street or Rugby carriage sidings but are maintained at Bletchley, near Milton Keynes, under contract with Network SouthEast. Early and late services are used to move the units from Birmingham to Rugby and Bletchley. The arrangements will be extended for the CrossCity Class 323 units. NSE's Class 321/4 EMUs are also regular visitors to Birmingham New Street providing a stopping service to and from London, whilst primarily for customers north of Northampton and Rugby. For this service Regional Railways Central sponsor four of the NSE Class 321 fleet.

Following the CrossCity (North) electrification **Tyseley** had 9 diagrams for twin-power units formed of Classes 101, 108 and 116. Rediagramming will allow all but Class 101 to be withdrawn as the last Class 153s, refurbished Class 101s and EMUs for the area become available. These are generally lightly diagrammed to work some services between Matlock and Derby. They also work between Crewe and Derby and some thence to Nottingham and Skegness. From Coventry the units are booked to Nuneaton and forward to Stafford and Stoke or Leicester or Nottingham and Lincoln Central. Other duties are Leicester–Nottingham, Rugby–Crewe via Coventry and Stoke-on-Trent and Shrewsbury–Wolverhampton.

Four Class 115 four-car units are diagrammed to peak period services on the CrossCity line. They are supplemented by 16 diagrams for Class 116, 117, 118 and 119 three-car units which include work between Birmingham New Street–Coventry–Leicester or Nottingham and Birmingham–Walsall–Wolverhampton. Of these some Class 117s will be retained, seven on ScotRail duties, having undergone recent refurbishment, but all other designs should be withdrawn by May 1993.

A much larger fleet of conventional DMUs has been disposed of following introduction of 27 Class 153 single cars to cover 23 diagrams. They have a wide area of operation, sometimes in pairs or in multiple with other Sprinter units to provide extra capacity on peak period services and move them between Tyseley and the country areas of operation. Long distance duties are from Birmingham New Street to Newark and Lincoln, Birmingham International to Wolverhampton and Aberystwyth, Derby or Doncaster to Boston and Skegness,

Sheffield–Lincoln–Peterborough and Sheffield–Retford–Cleethorpes. Less demanding duties are Wolverhampton–Chester, Leamington Spa–Stratford-on-Avon, Cleethorpes–Barton-on-Humber, Derby–Matlock, Stourbridge Town–Stourbridge Junction and Worcester–Barnt Green.

Centro require Regional Railways to operate a series of local trains in the area and, to their credit, have opted to fund the Class 150 Sprinter design above the more basic Pacers used elsewhere. Centro have also funded interior improvements to the two three-car Class 150 prototypes, 12 Class 150/1 units each with the addition of a Class 150/2 vehicle and 23 other two-car Class 150/1 and 150/2 units. There are 12 diagrams for three-car and 19 for two-car units of which some venture beyond the Centro area boundaries as through services and balancing workings. It should be made clear that Centro only fund the proportion of usage within the West Midlands PTE area. On weekdays they have only occasional duties on the CrossCity (Lichfield Trent Valley–Redditch) line but more extensively on Saturdays and all Sunday duties until May 1993. Many destinations are served from Birmingham New Street – primarily Derby, Great Malvern, Hednesford, Hereford, Nottingham, Nuneaton, Shirley, Walsall, Wolverhampton and Worcester. Lack of capacity at New Street leaves a few trains using the former Great Western terminus at Snow Hill for services to Dorridge, Great Malvern, Henley in Arden, Hereford, Leamington Spa, Shirley and Stratford-on-Avon. Other occasional duties are Birmingham International–Wolverhampton–Chester, Great Malvern–Oxford; and on Sundays Nottingham–Leamington Spa. Three-car sets only are diagrammed on the Shrewsbury–Pwllheli service.

Tyseley has a fleet currently of just four Class 156 units which have diagrams combined with five Class 150/2 units. The duties covered are the main Regional Railways Birmingham – Nuneaton – Leicester – Derby and Birmingham–Nottingham–Lincoln Central services with other duties between Leamington–Coventry–Lincoln, Newark Northgate–Lincoln, Lincoln–Sleaford, Nottingham–Skegness and Matlock–Derby–Crewe.

Derby Etches Park maintains 15 Class 156 Sprinter units and a modest fleet of hauled coaching stock, but by the summer 1993 reorganisation, following CrossCity electrification, Tyseley will have the capacity to maintain these. The Sprinters operate many services to Birmingham which will allow diagrams to be amended relatively easily. Duties from Derby, Nottingham, Oakham, Leicester, Tamworth HL, Chester, Aberystwyth, Pwllheli, Hereford and Worcester are all included. Elsewhere they work Worcester Foregate Street–Oxford, Lincoln–Crewe, Lincoln – Nuneaton – Coventry, Cleethorpes – Doncaster – Lincoln – Peterborough, Cleethorpes–Newark and Sheffield–Lincoln–Peterborough services.

The summer 1993 relief services were finalised as we went to press. Three eight-coach sets are to be involved in Cambrian Coast services and services from Birmingham to Great Yarmouth and Yarmouth to Nottingham on Saturdays and from Nottingham to Skegness on Mondays to Fridays. During the winter season they may be called on to deputise for DMU shortages and on some charter duties.

The East Anglia local services are operated from stock maintained at **Crown Point, Norwich** InterCity depot. The depot has to provide nine sets from its fleet of 13 Class 101s, although one duty is a spare at Colchester, ostensibly to cover the unit on NSE's Marks Tey–Sudbury branch. This service is expected to be operated by a Class 156 from May 1993 and could then provide a relief working between Norwich and/or Ipswich and Colchester to generate revenue when not in use on the branch. From Norwich the two-car Class 101 units are diagrammed to Ely, Great Yarmouth via Acle or Reed, Lowestoft, Cromer and Sheringham.

Duties from Ipswich are to Felixstowe, Bury St Edmunds and Cambridge. These duties should be taken over by single-car Class 153s from May 1993.

Crown Point currently operates six Class 156 diagrams from a fleet of seven units. The Ipswich–Saxmundham–Lowestoft line is signalled by Radio Electronic Token Block and thus restricted to suitably equipped trains. All seven Class 156s are so fitted which allows maximum use of the fleet without specific maintenance spare sets. From Norwich the units serve Cambridge, Ipswich, Lowestoft and Sheringham. Units reach Nottingham on duties from Ipswich and Stansted Airport. Other duties from Ipswich are services to Cambridge and Felixstowe.

South Wales and West

This is another area to have undergone an extensive change of Rolling Stock.

Cardiff Canton is the sole depot for the division's Express fleet and all South and West Wales local service rolling stock. Nine single-car Class 153 Sprinters have eight diagrams. These cover the long journey from Swansea and Llanelli via Llandovery, Llandrindod Wells, Craven Arms, Shrewsbury and Crewe; also most duties from Swansea to Pembroke Dock and Milford Haven. On some peak period services the West Wales diagrams provide capacity strengthening for Class 150 or Class 158 units.

The Cardiff Valley lines to Aberdare, Merthyr Tydfil, Treherbert and Rhymney and south to Penarth and Barry Island are shared amongst 25 Class 143 Pacers, 21 diagrams, and 26 Class 150 Sprinters, 21 diagrams. Coryton–Bute Road and Cardiff–Maesteg lines are Class 143s. Both designs are diagrammed to operate Cardiff Central–Bristol Temple Meads. The Pacers work local services from Bristol Temple Meads to Bath Spa, Weston-super-Mare, Taunton, Severn Beach and Gloucester also from Cardiff Central to Cheltenham Spa, Chepstow and Gloucester. Canton Sprinters also operate from Cardiff to Bath Spa and Shrewsbury; and from Bristol Temple Meads to Frome, Southampton, Weston-super-Mare and Weymouth.

Laira, Plymouth, is primarily an IC125 depot but caters for all local Regional Railways duties west of Taunton as well as any between-duty servicing of Cardiff based Express units. The conventional DMU fleet comprises five single car Class 122 units, and temporarily two Class 116 twin power-car units to cover technical problems. The Class 122s have three diagrams to cover the Liskeard–Looe, St Erth–St Ives and Par–Newquay branches. Some of the St Ives line services run through to Penzanze. A unit also works from Par–Liskeard after overnight servicing at St Blazey. and occasional Par–Newquay duties. They have no weekend duties.

Nine single-car Class 153s are based here, for seven diagrams, and are booked to cover the above duties on Saturdays. From Plymouth they have duties east to Exeter and west to Liskeard. From Exeter St Davids they cover duties to Barnstaple, Exmouth and Paignton. Two of the diagrams are centred on Bristol with duties from Temple Meads to Gloucester, Severn Beach and Taunton; also Swindon–Gloucester–Cheltenham and Westbury–Southampton services.

A fleet of 15 Class 150/2 Sprinters cover 13 diagrams. They also have duties in the Plymouth, Exeter and Bristol areas. On the main line they work local services to Penzance supplementing the InterCity and Regional Railways Express trains. Local diagrams are the Plymouth–Gunnislake branch and Truro–Falmouth Docks branches. Services between Paignton–Newton Abbot–Exmouth, Exeter Central–Taunton–Weston-super-Mare–Bristol Temple Meads and occasionally through to Gloucester or Severn Beach and Exeter Central–Barnstaple form a second group. Some local services between Bristol Temple Meads and Swindon are diagrammatically linked with duties from both stations to Gloucester and Worcester Shrub Hill.

ScotRail Express Class 158 No.158713 passes Inverkeithing on a service from the north for Edinburgh.
Brian Morrison

Interior view of a Class 158 coach. Seating is 2+2 almost throughout.
Brian Morrison

West Yorkshire PTE Class 158/9 Express unit No.158904 seen on a Liverpool Lime Street–Middlesbrough service in June 1992.
Barry Nicolle

Cyclic diagrams for North Wales coast services involve multiple working of different classes. Express unit No.158757 is headed by Class 156 No.156440 on a Llandudno-Manchester Victoria service on 27th June 1992. *Brian Morrison*

Regional Railways has ten two-car 400hp engined Class 158 units based at Cardiff, but they do not have dedicated duties and are therefore interchangeable in operation with the 350hp engined fleet. No.158866 is seen at Salisbury on 24th May 1992 forming the 10.05 Westbury–Portsmouth Harbour service. *Dave Titheridge*

ScotRail operates 16 Class 150/2 Sprinter units, mainly on Edinburgh Fife Circle duties, and maintained at Haymarket, Edinburgh, depot. No.150258 is seen approaching Edinburgh Waverley on a Fife Circle service on 13th June 1992. *Bill Wilson*

With sponsorship from Strathclyde PTE, most local services around Glasgow are operated by electric multiple units. In recent years a modified interior version of an NSE train has been purchased. In this view Class 318 unit No.318269, a three-car version of NSE's Class 317, is seen departing from Glasgow Central on an Ayr service. *Brian Morrison*

The oldest ScotRail EMUs, Class 303, were introduced in 1959, although of much more modern appearance including sliding doors. Used on North and South Clyde services they have been modified with gangways within each three-car unit to provide added safety and ease duties for revenue protection staff. Nos.303073, on a Newton service, and 303010 on a Cathcart Circle duty are seen waiting departure from Glasgow Central. *Brian Morrison*

Originally called the 'Glasgow Blue Trains', to accord with a livery chosen to match BR's Scottish Region marketing colour, Class 303 No.303048 has been restored to virtually original style, apart from small safety enhancements. The unit is seen at Bowling on a special duty in March 1991. *Brian Morrison*

A shortage of DMUs until recently left most Aberdeen–Inverness services locomotive hauled using Class 47/6s hired from InterCity. No.47677 heads such a service near Port Elphinstone. The former NSE & InterCity owned various liveried coaches now carry Regional Railways colours. Class 37/4 traction took over these duties from October 1992. *Cyril Loftus*

North Clyde Class 320 unit No.320320 passes Bowling with an Airdrie–Balloch service on 5th June 1992. *Bill Wilson*

The peak summer period 'Highland Heritage' train is seen approaching Lochluichart on its Inverness-Kyle of Lochalsh service on 4th August 1992. Note the coaches painted in Regional Railways (ScotRail) and Heritage liveries. *Cyril Loftus*

Strathclyde PTE livery surprisingly re-appeared on conventional DMUs late in 1992. Class 101 refurbished unit No.101684 is seen passing Corkerhill on a Paisley Canal–Glasgow Central service in November of that year. *Bill Wilson*

Tyne and Wear PTE sponsor some of the North East, Newcastle area, operated Class 142s and these are being painted in the distinctive bright yellow livery. Unit No.142020 is seen on a Middlesbrough–Hexham service at Newcastle in December 1992. *Brian Morrison*

Left The first of the production series Railbuses, the narrow-bodied Class 141, is generally restricted to country lines in West Yorkshire. No.141116 is seen approaching Poppleton with a York–Leeds service.
Barry Nicolle

Right Provincial liveried Pacer No.142091 departs from Leeds on a Scunthorpe service.
Brian Morrison

One of ten Class 144 units for which a third car had to be built to cover demand in the Leeds and Bradford area, No.144014 heads out of Keighley with a Skipton–Leeds service. The routes from Leeds and Bradford to Skipton and Ilkley are being electrified but a proposed order for 14 new Class 323 EMUs has not yet been placed owing to leasing problems connected with possible privatisation. *Barry Nicolle*

Some Class 142s units were painted chocolate and cream to work branch lines in Devon and Cornwall. They were unsuitable, now operate North East services and are being reliveried in Tyne & Wear PTE colours. Chocolate and cream No.142017 is seen at Colton Junction, York, on a local service to Hull. *Barry Nicolle*

The first Tyne & Wear liveried Class 142, No.142020, is seen on a Middlesbrough–Hexham service at Newcastle in December 1992. *Brian Morrison*

One of the Regional Railways North East Class 153 single cars, No.153317, is viewed at Bishop Auckland with a local service to Saltburn on 14th May 1991. These single engined cars provide a good standard of comfort on some medium distance, but lightly used, rural routes connecting larger towns and cities. *Barry Nicolle*

Regional Railways North West has a few Class 31/4s painted in its business colours to match the Mk2 coaching stock. A shortage of quality DMUs means that the locomotives and coaches are always busy during the summer months with services to holiday resorts. Nos.31410 and 31439 head a Llandudno–Crewe via Chester service. *Bob Casselden*

Thirteen Class 31/4s are operated by Regional Railways North West, although some will be replaced by the more powerful Class 37/4s as they are released from the freight sectors. Most carry the old Rail Blue livery, such as Nos.31442 and 31438 seen heading a Blackpool North–Manchester Victoria commuter service at Bolton on 6th July 1992. *Bob Casselden*

A mixture of old DMUs can still be found in the Manchester area although only Class 101s will survive by mid-1993. A recently refurbished unit in the smart business colours is seen at Manchester Piccadilly on a New Mills Central service. *Bob Casselden*

Regional Railways Class 142 unit No.142023 seen at Walsden, near Todmorden on a test run. This Manchester based train is the only example of the class carrying the Sector colours, lack of funding having deferred further repaints for the time being. *Bob Casselden*

Right Merseyrail Class 507 and 508 EMUs are being repainted in a new livery at major overhaul, the first time the local authority has had its trains in special colours. Painting the full fleet in these colours is likely to take a further nine years unless specially funded! No.507021 is seen at Southport in April waiting its next duty to Liverpool. Some Class 150 units are due for similar painting in 1994. *Bob Casselden*

The new Greater Manchester PTE livery is being applied to Class 150 units within that local authority's operating sponsorship. No.150133 stands in Stockport Carriage Sidings between duties on the Buxton line. *Bob Casselden*

Liveries on Class 150 Sprinters are somewhat varied. Seven Manchester based units are painted in Network NorthWest colours, a title applied before the North West area became an official separate business. No.150203 leaves Manchester Victoria on a Barrow service.

The Greater Manchester PTE sponsors some Class 142 Pacers for duties around the area. The first 14 units have spent all their life allocated to Newton Heath, Manchester, depot for this work and carry the sponsor's orange livery. Unit Nos.142005 and 142003 are seen at Rainhill with a Liverpool Lime Street–Manchester Victoria local service. *Bob Casselden*

Three-car augmented Class 150/1 unit No.150146 in Regional Railways colours stands at Wigan North Western forming a Liverpool Lime Street service in July 1992. The main duties for the area's six three-car units are Buxton–Blackpool North and Hazel Grove–Southport in line with peak traffic flows. Many standard two-car Class 150 Sprinter units are also available for semi-fast medium distance duties in the North West Division. *Bob Casselden*

The Barrow–Carlisle Cumbrian coast route via Workington and Whitehaven is usually operated by a single Class 153 vehicle. Although serviced at each end of the line they are maintained at Newton Heath, Manchester, and are usually worked in passenger service at quiet periods between Barrow and Manchester Victoria as part of a booked cyclic diagram.

Two classes of similar external appearance are Classes 304 and 305. The former are still in use on North West and Central services although most are due to be replaced as Class 323 units are delivered during 1993. Crew traction driving knowledge restricts the North West owned Class 305s to duties between Crewe and Manchester Piccadilly/Liverpool Lime Street. *Bob Casselden*

Above left Great Western Railway livery adorns Tyseley,
Birmingham, based Class 117 DMU set No.T305, seen at
Shrewsbury with a local service to Wolverhampton. Whilst most
trains are expected to carry their operating business or sponsor
colours, exceptions are occasionally made for historical reasons.
Any additional cost is usually recovered with requests for enthusiast
specials at weekends. *Brian Morrison*

Above Regional Railways refurbished Class 101 units are being
painted in the current business colours. Set No.101655 is seen
arriving at Cambridge with a local duty from Norwich.
Brian Morrison

Left Some coaches based at Derby still carry the very smart
Trans-Pennine colours applied for their former duties on the
Newcastle–Liverpool service, a livery to which the current Regional
Railways standard owes much. Mk2b TSO No.5453 is one of the
vehicles still in use. *Brian Morrison*

The West Midlands PTE has a marketing title 'Centro' carried on its buses and trains. Tyseley depot maintains 14 three-car and 23 two-car Class 150 series Sprinter units in the bright green and yellow colour scheme for their wide area of operation across the Midlands and to the Cambrian Coast. WMPTE only sponsors operations within its boundaries and some of the trains are financed by Regional Railways Central Division. No.150116 is seen at Dorridge. *Brian Morrison*

The first Class 323 EMU for Centro (West Midlands PTE) emerged from the Leeds factory of Hunslet TPL on 16th September 1992, following which it underwent extensive type approval testing at the Engineering Development Unit, RTC Derby, and running trials between Bletchley and Stafford. The unit is seen at Bletchley in December 1992. *Brian Morrison*

Interior of a Centro Class 323. *Brian Morrison*

Class 143 units have taken over many South Wales Valley lines. No.143621 is seen at Radyr with a Barry Island–Pontypridd service in March 1992. *Dave Titheridge*

Local services between Bristol and Southampton are now booked for Cardiff based Class 150/2 Sprinter units. No.150267 is seen near Southampton in May 1992. *Dave Titheridge*

Single car Class 153 units are the most economic answer to the scenic Heart of Wales line. No.153308 passes Whitchurch (Salop) with the Crewe–Swansea service. *Brian Morrison*

Class 122 single car No.55012 is seen at Laira depot. BR has not found any suitable new alternative for some of the tightly curved and steep Cornish branches. *Colin Marsden*

The most modern long distance EMU is the Class 442 Wessex Electric. Bournemouth maintains 24 units for 21 duties, careful diagramming allowing use on main services from both Weymouth and Portsmouth Harbour to Waterloo. Unit No.2421 is seen leaving Poole on 19th June 1992 on a Waterloo–Weymouth service. *Brian Morrison*

NETWORK SOUTHEAST

This Sector is responsible for most suburban routes in a general area within 80 miles of London. It operates a number of sub-businesses – Great Eastern, West Anglia, Thames & Chiltern, North London, Thameslink, South Central, South East, South West. The titles are general and, as the emblems on the side of rolling stock show, a variety of route brandings apply.

Almost all working by the business for passenger carrying trains is by diesel or electric multiple units, as so many lines south of the Thames were electrified by the Southern Railway and its constituent companies. From July 1992 the only booked locomotive-hauled regular services were on the West of England route where new Class 159 Express DMUs should be fully introduced by July 1993. Only a few hauled coaches may then be retained by NSE for special duties.

Several routes operated by NSE stock in fact extend beyond the official business boundary. In these instances appropriate funding is provided by InterCity or Regional Railways.

Great Eastern

This business centres on lines to the north east of Liverpool Street, including branches. All but one short route have overhead electrification. The main Norwich line is NSE territory to Manningtree ($59^1/_2$ miles) while many NSE services run as far as Ipswich, particularly supplementing the InterCity service during peak periods. At Manningtree the branch to Harwich leaves the main line. Parkeston Quay used to have a very busy freight business, but this is now mainly restricted to automotive traffic, as Felixstowe now has the main Freightliner terminal in the area. InterCity operates two trains daily between Parkeston Quay and London, and NSE runs a semi–fast service to London and a local service between Manningtree and Harwich Town. The NSE services are formed of Class 321 EMUs. At Colchester a route branches off to the coastal resort of Clacton, also a further junction at Thorpe-le-Soken for Walton-on-Naze.

These services are formed of a mix of Clacton-based units: 17 Class 309 (Essex Express), 35 x 312, and eight x 321/4. Outer suburban services to Chelmsford, Witham, Braintree and Colchester are also formed from the fleet of Class 312 units.

Shenfield is 20 miles from London and forms the boundary for inner suburban services. It is also a junction on the main line, the 'up' line crossing the Southend Victoria route by flyover. There are two separate routes to Southend, this line serving Billericay, Wickford and Rayleigh. The London, Tilbury and Southend route is referred to below. The only connection between the two routes runs between Forest Gate (GE) and Barking (LTS) and scheduled passenger services use this only during diversions off the latter route to/from Liverpool Street. Empty stock workings also use the route when necessary to reach the special facilities at Ilford Level 5 (heavy maintenance) Depot. The Southminster branch connects with the Southend Victoria line at Wickford and during peak periods has through services to/from Liverpool Street. The busy Southend commuter line has a fleet of 62 Class 321/3 units based at Ilford (Level 4) Depot, many running in three-unit formations.

The East London and East Essex commuter belt also requires 47 Class 315 inner suburban units, also based at Ilford. These primarily operate stopping services between Liverpool Street, Gidea Park and Shenfield. A few Southend stopping services also use these units, generally at the beginning or end of the day, in order to make use of overnight servicing facilities at Southend. One of these units operates throughout the day on the Romford–Upminster branch – no track connection exists at Upminster with the LTS or London Underground.

There is an easy customer interchange at both ends of the line.

Many suburban services call at Stratford which provides a useful cross-platform link with Central Line services to/from the City and with the Docklands Light Railway. A low level Stratford station forms part of the North London Line route between North Woolwich (connection with Woolwich free ferry across the Thames) and Richmond to connect with NSE's South Western lines.

Reference was made above to one non-electrified line operated by the Great Eastern business. This is just a 12 mile, 20 minute, journey from Marks Tey – the London side of Colchester – to Sudbury operated by Class 101 DMUs, serviced at Colchester and from October 1992 maintained by Regional Railways at Norwich. An agreement between the two businesses is expected to see a Class 156 provided for this service from May 1993. Just three miles down the line from Marks Tey is Chappel and Wakes Colne, home of the Stour Valley Railway Preservation Society.

London, Tilbury & Southend line

This is the North Thames line with a very substantial commuter traffic but lack of post-1958 electrification investment has led to its being regarded as the 'misery line'. It runs from London, Fenchurch Street, to Barking (interchange with London Underground), Upminster, Southend Central and Shoeburyness. A branch leaves the main line at Barking for Dagenham Dock and Tilbury. Riverside Station (connecting with a ferry crossing to Gravesend) closed in November 1992 to be replaced by a bus link from Tilbury Town. From Tilbury a loop is completed via Stanford le Hope to rejoin the main line at Pitsea. The town of Ockendon is served by a link service between Upminster and Tilbury. Stock for the line varies from 24 of the original Class 302s, although now refurbished with through gangways and open saloon accommodation, with only the former First Class area in compartments with side corridor. Also over 30 years old are the line's 38 Class 308 units. The 43 Class 310/0 units were built in 1965 for Euston–Northampton services and 15 Class 312, built in 1975/76 for Clacton line services, complete the passenger train fleet for the route. All units are maintained at East Ham depot.

NSE was planning to spend £50million on the line's infrastructure – track and signalling – during 1993-94; however, this cannot now be funded from current resources and any badly needed modern replacement rolling stock awaits negotiation between the BRB and the Government. May 1997 is now seen as the earliest and even then it is likely to be a combination of 'second–hand' Class 315, 317 or 321 units.

Fenchurch Street is a very short walk from Tower Hill (London Underground) and Tower Gateway (Docklands) stations.

West Anglia

This business has four main routes from Liverpool Street, all with a very busy commuter traffic. However the pride of the line has to be the 'Stansted Express' service run in conjunction with British Airways and which showed a profit in its first year of operation. A half hourly interval express service runs daily from Liverpool Street to Stansted Airport using four of the five Class 322 units. The service calls only at Tottenham Hale, to connect with the London Underground Victoria Line and hourly at Bishops Stortford as a connection to/from Lea Valley line stations, branching off the Cambridge main line just beyond Stansted Mountfitchet. Occasionally the service is diverted from Hackney Downs via the Southbury loop line to Cheshunt in which case it connects with London Underground's Victoria Line at Seven Sisters instead of Tottenham Hale. As Stansted becomes even more important as London's third airport it is possible that an enhanced rail service will be required, although expansion of the

Thameslink network, planned for the year 2000, may cover this. The Class 322 units, being technically identical to Class 321, are maintained at Ilford.

The main Cambridge services routed via Tottenham and Bishops Stortford are operated by 33 Class 317 units based at Hornsey. Class 321 units have operated this line but are not now so allocated.

The two lines which formed the 'Jazz' from Liverpool Street in steam days, those to Enfield Town via Seven Sisters and to Chingford via Walthamstow are normally formed by 15 Class 315 units. The latter route is supplemented in the peak period by the remaining 12 original 1960 built Class 305 EMUs. A similar stock situation applies to Southbury loop line services to Cheshunt, Broxbourne and Hertford East. Six Class 302 units are provided by East Ham (see LTS above) for Chingford and Hertford line duties. NSE is due to eliminate all Class 305 stock by end of March 1993 when six Class 313 units will be cascaded from Great Northern services as replacements. Slight service adjustments will be necessary, although mainly achieved by shortening formations on the shoulder services of peak periods.

Alternative services for Enfield, Hertford and Cambridge use the Great Northern lines from King's Cross.

Thameslink

A fleet of 60 Class 319/0 (Standard Class only) and 26 Class 319/1 units (First & Standard class) operate this cross-London service which at peak periods is at full capacity. In fact the congestion in the London Bridge area precludes operation of the full service desired by NSE. The present King's Cross Thameslink station entrance has to be closed for a few minutes during some evening peak periods to allow platforms to clear safely. The BRB has major plans to expand and improve the service by the end of this decade by adding an extra line through the London Bridge area and building a replacement Thameslink station in a major redevelopment of the King's Cross and St Pancras stations area including a Channel Tunnel London terminal. Both schemes await further extensive negotiations between BRB and the Government.

The service effectively is in two halves - the northern part from Bedford, serving Luton, St Albans and Cricklewood to King's Cross Thameslink. In the peak some services use St Pancras main line terminus or after Farringdon divert to Moorgate for City customers. These routes are operated on the 25kV AC overhead system. Trains continuing south of the river lower their pantographs and third-rail collection shoes at Farringdon to proceed on 750V DC to City Thameslink (formerly St Pauls) [closed on Sundays] and Blackfriars. For normal operation the two platforms for Thameslink are sufficient. Blackfriars station has also a number of terminal platforms normally used by South Eastern services to and from Kent.

The original Thameslink service then proceeded via London Bridge and East Croydon via Gatwick Airport and Three Bridges to Brighton. Many Brighton travellers had been used to First Class facilities and resented NSE's policy of dropping this, although the St Pancras–Bedford trains had not had this option for many years! However, NSE made temporary arrangements on the Class 319/0 units used on key commuter services until the second series units arrived as part of the route's expansion. Now Class 319/1 units are diagrammed to some services on the South Central Sussex Coast main line.

The expansion introduced through trains from north of the Thames to the Kent destinations of Bromley South and Sevenoaks with a few to Orpington; and in Surrey to Epsom and Guildford with a peak period service via Blackfriars to Wimbledon and Sutton.

All Thameslink units are based at Selhurst (Level 4) Depot for maintenance.

The potential for express Thameslink services from King's Lynn, Cambridge, Peterborough and Bedford to Ramsgate, Hastings, Brighton and Portsmouth, also north of Bedford if electrified, is considerable. Sadly that is at least a few years away.

Great Northern

Fitting in very busy inner and outer suburban commuter services between numerous East Coast main line trains timed at 125mph is no easy task but is achieved with a high degree of reliability. At the main King's Cross terminus NSE has its own four platform station although some services use the adjacent eight InterCity platforms, fully justified as the NSE northern boundary is Huntingdon, while a frequent service operates all day to Peterborough.

From Hitchin what was previously a branch line to commuter towns of Letchworth and Royston and subsequently had electrification extended. to Cambridge, is now regarded as the premier route between the university town and the capital because of the shorter journey time possible. In August 1992 the service was extended deep into East Anglia with electrification from Cambridge to Ely and King's Lynn, thus reinstating the through trains to the capital and significantly increasing the service to the Norfolk port. A fleet of 39 Class 317 units is currently allocated to the King's Cross–Peterborough/Cambridge/ King's Lynn circuit.

Some outer suburban stopping services to/from Peterborough diverge from the main line between Stevenage and Welwyn Garden City to serve Watton-at-Stone and Hertford North, then fast to Finsbury Park and King's Cross.

Inner suburban services are currently worked by a fleet of 44 Class 313 dual-voltage units. They form the stopping services from Hertford North and Welwyn Garden City to Finsbury Park and to Drayton Park to switch between AC and DC current, then forward to Moorgate. Late evening and weekend services operate to King's Cross instead of Moorgate. These units are also maintained at Hornsey.

North London and Northampton Lines

These businesses cover the inner and outer suburban routes from Euston using 20 Class 313 and 40 Class 321/4 units and various minor services, all stock being maintained at Bletchley.

The Euston–Watford Junction DC lines service is regarded as part of the North London lines. The branch from Watford Junction to Croxley Green has two morning and one mid-evening service only. Between Queens Park and Harrow & Wealdstone tracks are shared with London Underground's Bakerloo line. The Class 313 units do not normally work north of Watford, except to and from Bletchley depot – one of the rare uses of their AC overhead equipment.

Generally regarded as part of the same business, although technically allocated seven of the above Class 313 units of its own, is the 20min interval 67min all stations journey from North Woolwich via Stratford, Highbury & Islington, Gospel Oak and Willesden Junction to Richmond. Interchange is possible with many other BR and Underground routes along its 22$^1/_2$ mile journey, the section from Gunnersbury to Richmond sharing tracks with London Underground's District Line.

The Class 321/4 units operate at up to 100mph on the Euston–Northampton–Birmingham New Street semi-fast services, although are capable of higher speeds when specially required. As with the Great Northern, they have to mesh in with a busy InterCity service and while they leave the main line at Roade, just beyond Wolverton, they rejoin it for Rugby station when on journeys to Birmingham New Street in a joint operation with Regional Railways Central. InterCity's West Coast route is limited to 110mph; west of Rugby it is 100mph, but plans are being evaluated to increase speeds substantially when funds allow. In this case NSE will be pressured by InterCity to speed up its Northampton service, hopefully by modifying traction motors on existing stock. Network Express peak services usually call once only between Euston and Milton Keynes, with two running only between Euston and Bletchley calling at Leighton Buzzard. Such services are normally 12-car formations, while non-peak daily operation calls for four or eight-car rakes.

One unit, of either design, works the $6\frac{1}{2}$ mile Watford Junction–St Albans Abbey branch which has five intermediate halts.

The Three Counties line from Bletchley to Bedford St Johns is cleared for main line operation with IC125s or Mk3 loco–hauled trains for diversionary purposes between West Coast and Midland main lines (Bletchley–Bedford Midland). It has, however, a regular DMU service currently formed by Classes 108 and 115 two-car units. Bletchley maintains four to cover three diagrams. By April 1993 all services will be worked by Class 121 units; with peak duties, primarily for schools' customers, augmented by a two-car Class 117 unit.

Because it is a North London DMU service Bletchley also maintains the Gospel Oak–Barking trains. Old Oak Common would be a more convenient depot but the 'wrong' operating business 'owns' it. Thus three life-expired twin power-car Classes 108 and 115 units and three refurbished Class 117 units are currently allocated to the route to cover four diagrams. The life expired units will be replaced by further Class 117 units shortly.

The continuance of Bletchley as a depot for diesel maintenance is being reviewed as the Centro Class 323 units have been added to the depot's commitments. The problem of suitable alternative facilities and future rolling stock requires NSE's careful consideration. Tyseley (for Bedford line) and Reading (for Barking line) stock appear to be most likely although Willesden and Aylesbury cannot be ruled out.

Thames and Chiltern Lines
The Chiltern Lines have the once famous Great Central terminus of Marylebone at the London end serving west Hertfordshire and Buckinghamshire countryside. Although threatened with closure in the late 1980s Marylebone has been extensively modernised along with BR stations on the line to Aylesbury and Banbury and brand new trains introduced. The line is being used for trials of one of two systems of Automatic Train Protection (ATP) prior to national introduction as a technological advancement of the current national Advanced Warning System (AWS).

There are two routes from Marylebone to Aylesbury. The direct route is $37\frac{1}{2}$ miles via Harrow-on-the-Hill, Rickmansworth and Amersham. The $14\frac{1}{2}$ miles between Harrow-on-the-Hill and Amersham are jointly operated with London Underground's Metropolitan Line from London Baker Street and stations to Aldgate in the City of London. London Underground is responsible for infrastructure and staffing over the joint section. The other route is $43\frac{1}{2}$ miles via Wembley, Ruislip, High Wycombe and Princes Risborough. Marylebone–Banbury services take this route via Princes Risborough continuing via Bicester North, a total journey of $68\frac{3}{4}$ miles. New 75mph Class 165/0 diesel multiple units are allocated to this route, 28 two-car and seven three-car, with a further four three-cars on loan to Thames line, available for an improved service in due course.

The faster route to Banbury is the $86\frac{1}{2}$ miles Thames line from Paddington via Oxford, but served by through Network Express trains only in the peak period. Regular InterCity trains run between Reading and Birmingham. A fast regular service runs between Paddington and Oxford and less frequently between

Paddington and Newbury. These services changed between March and July 1992 from locomotive hauled trains to three- or six-car Class 165 formations. In the spring of 1993 the first of 21 new Class 166 three-car air-conditioned DMUs should be introduced on all the Thames line Network Express services, and from May some will be extended from Oxford to Birmingham Snow Hill in a joint arrangement with Regional Railways.

Local NSE services on the main line between Paddington–Reading–Didcot–Oxford are worked by a variety of stock. The winter timetable commenced with 17 three-car and ten Class 165/1 two-car units (including the three-car units lent to Express services). The full fleet of 37 two-car sets was available by the end of 1992. As the 21 three-car Class 166 units are delivered the three-car 165/1 units will join the suburban fleet. This will eliminate the mixture of Classes 101, 104, 108, 121 and primarily 117 units still maintained at Reading and Old Oak Common for the main line and branch services; excepting North Downs and Greenford lines where infrastructure clearances require attention.

The Paddington–Ealing Broadway–Greenford, Maidenhead–Bourne End–Marlow, Reading and Twyford–Henley-on-Thames and Slough–Windsor branches are usually now two-car units, the former scheduled for Class 117 power twins and the others for the mix of Class 101 and 108 units. Local services between Reading–Newbury–Bedwyn, Reading–Didcot–Oxford–Banbury and Oxford–Bicester Town are two-car diagrams but increasingly Class 165s are being substituted. All off-peak and weekend services on the main line should be Class 165 operated.

The former Great Western Reading–Basingstoke line is now operated by the NSE South Western Division but will become a joint service by next May. Reading-based Class 165s will operate Reading–Basingstoke locals and South Western Class 159s will operate the through Salisbury service.

On the other hand, the North Downs line, much of which is not yet electrified, is served from its western end using Reading-based three-car DMUs of Classes 101, 117, and 119. The line's operation is to be divided, probably from May 1993. The section from Reading–Wokingham–Guildford–Redhill, thence to Gatwick Airport will be operated initially by existing DMUs, but as soon as possible by Class 165s. The section from Redhill to Tonbridge will be operated by the South Eastern Division, initially with DEMUs, and later Class 411 EMUs following electrification work at present in hand.

South Eastern Division

One of the three divisions south of the River Thames, formerly Southern Region, the South Eastern uses Charing Cross as its main London terminus, also Blackfriars, Cannon Street and a significant part of Victoria to cover Kent Link inner suburban services and Kent Coast express and outer suburban duties.

The main route from London to the Kent Coast (Boat Train No.1) is from Charing Cross via London Bridge, Orpington, Tonbridge to Ashford, Folkestone and Dover Priory, then round the coast to Ramsgate. Some services run from Ashford via Canterbury West to Ramsgate.

Boat train route No.2 is from Victoria (Eastern) via Bromley (South), Gillingham (Kent), Faversham and Canterbury East to Dover Western Docks. Other services from Victoria travel east from Faversham via Margate to Ramsgate.

Maidstone East is served by many trains from London to Ashford. Victoria services are semi-fast or all stations via Bromley South, Otford and Malling while Charing Cross is the terminus for fast services.

Medway Valley line services call at all stations between Strood and Paddock Wood via Maidstone West. Main line services are not booked over this line.

The main route from London to Hastings is from Charing Cross via Tonbridge, Tunbridge Wells and St Leonards. An alternative route is via the Central Division from Victoria. Occasional services between Charing Cross and the Kent Coast are routed via Dartford and Gillingham.

Rolling stock for Kent Coast services is maintained at Ramsgate, and serviced at other depots such as Dover, Grove Park and Victoria. The fleet comprises 121 Class 411 4-CEP, 13 Class 421/4 4-CIG, and 61 Class 423 4-VEP units covering 167 diagrams plus six Class 415/7 units for peak hour duties with cover from the Class 411s. The fleet also includes five two-car Class 414/3 units as cover. The Class 421 units normally form part of the Hastings line fleet. Boat Trains are usually the Class 411 units.

The Hastings to Ashford line via Rye, The Marshes Link, not electrified, uses the three two-car Class 207/1 diesel electric multiple units and the gangwayed Class 205/1 unit.

Kent Link suburban services are in the process of major modernisation which, on present orders, will comprise 147 four-car Class 465 (15 in traffic at mid-January 1993) and 43 two-car Class 466 units. The intention is that these will replace all the current fleet – 21 Class 413 and 116 Class 415 four-car and 61 Class 416 two-car units. New Class 465 units were introduced on services between Cannon Street and Charing Cross to Dartford routed via Woolwich, Sidcup or Bexleyheath, also services to Orpington, Sevenoaks, Gravesend and Hayes from the end of November 1992. Over 30 more Class 465 units from the two manufacturers were undergoing acceptance trials and driver training at the time of writing and more were complete at GEC Metro-Cammell's Washwood Heath factory. The first Class 466 unit was delivered by GEC to the Railway Technical Centre, Derby on 23rd December 1992 for type testing. They will initially displace Class 415 units of both types, with those in poorest mechanical and bodywork condition being withdrawn first.

However, while initially it will not be possible to increase the current maximum 10-coach formations, station platforms are being extended to allow 12-car rakes to be introduced. This requires major works at Woolwich and complete resignalling and station extension at Dartford. Current suburban services are operated as 4-, 6-, 8- or 10-car formations according to the time of day. With the exception of two coaches of the preserved Class 415/1 unit and half coach portions of Class 416/2 units all non-internal gangway (ie closed compartment) stock has been condemned. These units do not have corridor connections between vehicles. The new stock has gangways within each two- or four-car unit.

Charing Cross Kent Link services run via London Bridge, Lewisham, Woolwich Arsenal or Bexleyheath and Dartford to Gravesend and Gillingham, and via London Bridge, Greenwich and Woolwich Arsenal to Dartford; also to Dartford via Lewisham and Sidcup. Charing Cross is the terminus for services via Lewisham and Elmers End to Addiscombe and Hayes. Off-peak the Elmers End–Addiscombe branch is worked as a two-car shuttle. Charing Cross also runs services via Hither Green to Orpington and Sevenoaks.

Blackfriars–Orpington–Sevenoaks services run via Catford and Bromley South; off-peak these are part of the NSE Thameslink through trains from north of the River Thames.

Victoria–Sevenoaks Kent Link services are routed via Herne Hill and Bromley South. A few peak-period services run between Victoria, Lewisham, Bexleyheath and Dartford.

All stock for Kent Link services is maintained at Slade Green, near Dartford. To ease movements at the beginning and end of peak periods some services on the Bexleyheath line run directly to/from Slade Green instead of Dartford. Stock for

Kent Coast and Kent Link services is stabled and cleaned at the new Hither Green sidings where flushing aprons have been provided for the chemical retention toilets fitted to Networker trains. Stabling and servicing facilities are also provided at Grove Park and Gillingham.

Two-car shuttle services operate between Grove Park and Bromley North.

South Central Division

The London termini of Victoria and London Bridge share a comprehensive service on South London lines and Sussex Coast duties.

Through Thameslink services via London Bridge run to Gatwick Airport and Brighton and InterCity's Gatwick Express operates between Victoria and the airport station. These have been covered in earlier pages.

The main Sussex Coast duties from London's termini run vía East Croydon, Redhill, Gatwick Airport and Haywards Heath to Brighton, or after Haywards Heath run via Lewes to Newhaven and Seaford (peak periods) or Eastbourne and Hastings.

The line between Victoria and Gatwick Airport is also used by services for Crawley, Horsham, Bognor Regis and Chichester and Portsmouth Harbour. The latter station is better served from London by South Western Division (see below). A few services use the route via Horsham to Littlehampton. Littlehampton services from London mainly use the Brighton line to Haywards Heath, thence to Hove and Worthing where they divide, part going forward to Southampton (see South Western Division). Coastal services operate between Hastings and Brighton, Seaford and Brighton, Brighton and Littlehampton and Portsmouth Harbour.

These services are worked by a fleet of 88 Class 421 4-CIG units, 76 diagrams, and 46 Class 423 4-VEP units, 41 diagrams, all based at Brighton. The Class 421s are mainly used on longer distance trips and filling in duties on shorter journeys. The Class 423 units are scheduled for stopping and shorter distance services. A fleet of seven Class 422/2 and 12 Class 422/3 4-BIG buffet car units have 15 diagrams on fast services between Victoria and Brighton, Hastings and Worthing or Littlehampton. Trolley catering is available on some other longer journeys.

Victoria–East Croydon–Oxted–East Grinstead services are the preserve of Class 423 units. The Oxted–Uckfield line is not electrified and is the only duty for 12 Selhurst-based, South London lines, Class 205 diesel electric multiple units.

South Central's suburban stock is all based at Selhurst. The fleet comprises just four refurbished Class 415/4 4-EPB units on three diagrams; 34 Class 416/3 2-EPB units, 30 diagrams; 46 Class 455/8 4-HIT units (one temporarily three-car), 36 diagrams and 24 new Class 456 units for 20 diagrams.

South London suburban services operating between Victoria and London Bridge via Clapham High Street or Streatham were using new Class 456 units during the summer but reverted to Class 416/3 units, presumably temporarily, at the beginning of the winter service.

Victoria or London Bridge – West Croydon, Victoria – Crystal Palace–Beckenham Junction services are usually formed of Class 415 or 416 stock.

Victoria or London Bridge – East Croydon – Smitham – Tattenham Corner, Victoria–Sutton–Epsom, Victoria–Sutton–London Bridge, Charing Cross (off-peak)–London Bridge–Caterham and West Croydon–Wimbledon trains are formed from the sliding door Class 455s. Class 319s also fill in on some Victoria–Epsom duties.

South Western Division

This division has the fastest trains south of the Thames, two 'tube' lines and the greatest involvement with InterCity services. The main service is Waterloo–

Southampton–Bournemouth–Poole–Weymouth using the Wessex Electric Class 442 units on fast and semi-fast services. The fleet of 24 five-car units is based at Bournemouth for 21 diagrams. Since the summer of 1992 the units have some duties off-peak on the Waterloo–Guildford–Portsmouth line, but they have to return to Bournemouth on alternate days for effluent treatment. Bournemouth is the only depot currently with facilities for normal maintenance on this fleet with BRML Eastleigh Works carrying out bogie changes and heavier repairs.

The Waterloo–Portsmouth service via Guildford also runs as fast and semi-fast usually with Eastleigh-based Class 412 4-BEP units, seven for five duties, and some of the Class 421/5 4-CIG 'Greyhound' units. Stopping services between Waterloo–Woking–Guildford–Portsmouth usually are formed of Class 423 4-VEP stock. Some Waterloo–Portsmouth through services (now routed over the recently electrified line between Eastleigh and Fareham), the Waterloo–Southampton stopping services, Waterloo–Reading and Waterloo–Ascot–Guildford duties are shared between Classes 421 and 423, sometimes working together.

Waterloo–Alton and Waterloo–Basingstoke stopping services and Brockenhurst–Lymington Pier (for Yarmouth, IoW) are formed of the Class 423 4-VEP stock.

The Class 421 4-CIG units, 42 for 36 diagrams including 'Greyhounds' are allocated to Eastleigh depot and the Class 423 4-VEP units, 82 for 74 diagrams, to East Wimbledon.

While InterCity operates the prime London–Exeter route, the former London and South Western (subsequently Southern Railway) line from Waterloo via Woking, Basingstoke, Salisbury and Yeovil Junction continues as a somewhat slower alternative route. The service has been beleaguered in recent years by locomotive availability problems due to dedicating specific locomotives, initially Class 50 and currently Old Oak Common based Class 47/7, to the route which combines fast running between London and Basingstoke with stop-start undulating line west of Salisbury. At times of poor availability NSE Class 33s, whose maximum speed of 85mph and power is insufficient for nine-coach trains, and Class 47 traction from Rail express systems is 'hired'. The coaches are mostly maintained at Old Oak Common with just two sets based at Eastleigh. Many of these coaches have reached the stage where life expiry is imminent without overhaul at unwarranted cost and a few coaches have been borrowed from Regional Railways summer service fleet as short term cover. This is due to change from the spring of 1993 as 22 new three-car Class 159 DMUs, 400hp Cummins engined version of the Class 158 but with both classes of seating, are delivered from ABB Transportation (BREL) Derby and modified to NSE specifications by Babcock Thorn at Rosyth Dockyard.

The new trains will be maintained at a purpose-built depot constructed at Salisbury and by the mid-summer of 1993 should have completely displaced locomotives and Mk2 coaches on scheduled NSE services. It is to be hoped that by this time all design gremlins discovered in the sister Regional Railways owned trains will have been eliminated and the intensive use on this arduous route will not identify more problems with these impressive looking trains.

The $15\frac{1}{2}$ mile link between Reading and Basingstoke, extensively used by InterCity Cross Country services, is not electrified and is generally operated at present by Eastleigh-based Classes 205 (two) and 207 (four) diesel electric multiple units (DEMU) for four diagrams of local shuttles. Most trains between Salisbury and Southampton form part of Regional Railways Western Express services calling only at Romsey or Sprinter stopping duties between Bristol and Southampton. NSE supplements these services with a DEMU between Salisbury and Southampton and also some through operations between Salisbury and

Reading via Basingstoke. The Reading–Basingstoke line is to be 'transferred' to Thames division operation next summer, with Class 165s replacing the DEMUs (see 'Thames' above).

A fleet of 91 Class 455 units is allocated to this division's 80 diagrammed London inner-suburban duties. These include Waterloo to Hounslow (including circular via Brentford/Richmond), Kingston, Staines, Weybridge, Windsor and Eton Riverside, Shepperton via Kingston or Richmond, Hampton Court, all-stations services to Guildford via Surbiton and Woking or Effingham Junction, Chessington South and Epsom via Wimbledon.

During peak periods a shuttle service operates between Clapham Junction and Kensington Olympia (London Underground now operates an all day service to Olympia from High St Kensington and Earls Court). The NSE service is forecast for expansion when the line's electrification for Channel Tunnel freight trains is completed. At the present time the line has continued with an Eastleigh-based Class 205 DEMU but a Class 455 will probably be used from late January 1993 when electrification and signalling work is completed.

South Western operates two self-contained routes with tube size stock necessary to fit line loading gauge. The Waterloo and City line – Waterloo–Bank – has a fleet of nine power cars and 12 trailers (eight + 12 diagrams), Class 485, usually formed into five-car trains maintained at their own depot below street level at Waterloo. On the rare occasions of moving stock to and from the line it is now necessary to use a crane. The former lift shaft was removed during works for building the Channel Tunnel terminus at Waterloo. During peak periods the line is used to its maximum capacity, but as the City has very little business on Saturday afternoons and Sundays the line is closed. Following major modernisation five new four-car Class 482 trains, to the same specification as ABB Transportation (BREL) are currently producing for London Underground's Central Line, should enter service in the spring of 1993.

The second 'tube' route at least operates in daylight and is more scenic, running from Ryde Pier Head to Shanklin, Isle of Wight. Nine two-car Class 483 units formed of rebuilt London Underground 1938 tube stock operate six diagrams and are maintained at Ryde St Johns Road depot. On occasions when stock has to be moved to or from the mainland a low-loader lorry takes the vehicle(s) between Fratton (Portsmouth) and Sandown for re-railing, as roads on the island are unsuitable for large road transporters to get to Ryde. Business on the Island line has increased with the opening of Smallbrook station, not road connected, solely to provide a connection with the Isle of Wight Steam Railway.

Charter

Network SouthEast does not have a significant fleet of Charter stock. When required it usually hires coaches from InterCity, including privately owned vehicles. However a few units have been restored as closely as possible to 'as built' condition, taking into consideration current safety requirements such as yellow warning panels and headlights. Two four-car Class 438 4-TC units require loco-motive haulage by either Classes 33/1 or 73 when in passenger service and thus are rarely used away from the former Southern Region. They can be driven from either end of the unit in a 'push-pull' mode. Other Class 33 locomotives can haul 'pull' them only, but very few have operational train heating equipment.

Other stock available is all self propelled. The preserved 4-EPB (Class 411) No.5001 and 4-SUB No.4732 are still owned by BR and able to work on the 750v DC lines. North of the Thames Ilford depot still looks after the Class 306 'Shenfield' unit No.017 for 25kv AC operation.

Three Class 50 locomotives are owned by by this business, used solely for enthusiast rail tours since retirement from normal service.

A line up of Class 313 units await their next duties from Watford to Euston on the suburban dc supply lines. From Harrow to Queens Park the line is shared with London Underground's Bakerloo line. *Brian Morrison*

A pair of Class 321/4 units, Nos.321404/03, arrive at Euston with a morning service from Bletchley. *Brian Morrison*

First generation DMUs are gradually disappearing from Thames line duties as new Network Turbos become available. In this view Class 117 unit No.L423 accelerates from Didcot, forming a stopping service for Oxford in February 1992. *Dave Titheridge*

A Paddington–Slough suburban service at West Ealing with Class 121 single power cars 55024/25 at front and rear respectively. This is now the only booked working for one of this class with NSE; the second is standing-in for a Class 117 power car. *Dave Titheridge*

The temporary order on NSE Thames Express duties, new Network Turbo No.165110 forms an Oxford–Paddington service at West Ealing on 11th June 1992 prior to the introduction of air conditioned Class 166 sister units on the services. *Dave Titheridge*

The Class 319/1 Thameslink units are easily identified by their white cab roofs. They differ from the original 60 in having a First Class seating area following complaints from Brighton line customers accustomed to the facility on all their other trains. *Brian Morrison*

Five Class 322 units, similar to Class 321 but with a higher standard of interior finish, are sponsored by BAA to provide four throughout the day on a 30min interval Liverpool Street–London Stansted Airport service. Unit No.322484 is seen calling at a refurbished Tottenham Hale, to connect with the London Underground Victoria Line to the West End, on 19th March 1992. *Brian Morrison*

The interior of the Class 322 is fully carpeted and upholstered in a green and grey style to match the special exterior livery. The special service has been very successful to a developing airport. On rare occasions standard Class 317 or 321 units deputise. *Brian Morrison*

West Anglia has 27 diagrams for Class 317 units on services from King's Lynn via Cambridge to Liverpool Street. The units are generally similar to the Great Northern units (King's Lynn via Cambridge, also Peterborough, to King's Cross) and are thus all maintained at Hornsey depot, north London. Unit No.317367 stands at Cambridge with magazines being unloaded before returning to Liverpool Street. *Brian Morrison*

A design well ahead of its time was this 1949 built 'Shenfield' unit, latterly BR Class 306. This preserved sliding door unit No.017 is available for private charter duties anywhere on the 25kv AC network. It is seen 'at home' on Ilford Depot. *Brian Morrison*

Top Class 321 units are the mainstay of Great Eastern services, capable of Driver Only Operation (DOO). All 66 of the first design and eight of the version with extra First Class seats for Northampton line services cover 63 diagrams daily on the routes from Liverpool Street to Southend Victoria and Clacton. Unit No.321329 coasts down Brentwood Bank with a Southend–Liverpool Street service. *Brian Morrison*

Above Great Eastern is unlikely to be fully DOO for some while and still operates 35 of the 1975-built slam-door Class 312 EMUs, with maintenance at Clacton. Unit No.312708 is seen heading through Brentwood with a Witham-bound service. *Brian Morrison*

The Clacton Express units were introduced in 1962 and most continue in front line service between London and the East Essex coast. The remaining fleet of 17 units cover 13 diagrams; a few have had to be withdrawn due to lack of unique spare components. There is no current plan to replace these veterans. Unit No.309622 is seen leaving Colchester on 29th July 1992 with a Clacton-bound service. *Brian Morrison*

The mainstay of the LT&S for over 30 years has been the Class 302. Those remaining have a few more years to soldier on. No.302217 is seen leaving Fenchurch Street. *Brian Morrison*

The Mk2 coach design of Class 310 units gives a more modern appearance to the LT&S, but these units started life on the Euston-Northampton line where their 75mph top speed is no longer sufficient. No.310064 arrives at Fenchurch Street from Tilbury. *Brian Morrison*

One of the dual voltage Class 313 units noted on Holloway Bank on a King's Cross–Welwyn Garden City duty. Only late evening and weekend duties normally take these units into King's Cross, at other times they leave the main line at Finsbury Park for Moorgate. *Brian Morrison*

Class 423/0 unit No.3139 heads a Littlehampton–Victoria service at Horsham on 16th June 1992. Units with extra seating and a reduced van area are classified 423/1 numbered 34xx and 35xx. *Dave Titheridge*

Class 422/2 unit No.2204 provides the buffet facilities on this Victoria–Hastings service passing Clapham Junction. A buffet is the only catering service provided today on the South Coast trains — a far cry from the days of the Brighton Belle. *Brian Morrison*

Central provides a South London link service between Victoria and London Bridge. These are worked by the new Class 456 units (based on the Class 321 design). No.456017 is seen at Wandsworth Road on 27th July. *Brian Morrison*

Above The outer-suburban Class 423 vehicles are still widely used on the South Eastern Division. Approximately 55 units are used daily, mainly on services from Kent to the London termini. Class 423/0 unit No.3163 is seen emerging from its home depot, Ramsgate, to form a semi-fast service to Victoria. *Brian Morrison*

CAP units were formed by combining two HAP units and whilst the intermediate cabs remained, driving controls were made non-operational. Class 413 Nos.3203/02 pass Bromley South on a Victoria–Ramsgate duty. *Brian Morrison*

A three-car Class 159 made its debut in London on 31st July 1992 when forming a demonstration special for NSE management. It is seen at Clapham Cutting on its run from Salisbury–Waterloo. Service introduction was scheduled for spring 1993. *Brian Morrison*

Interior of Class 159, First Class. Note the 2+1 seating compared with Class 158 style. *Brian Morrison*

The Kent Link Networker units come in three forms from two manufacturers. Two are four-car — Class 465/0 from ABB Transportation (formerly BREL) and Class 465/2 from GEC Alsthom (Metro-Cammell works) — and two-car Class 466 also from GEC. It is intended that 12-car formations of any combination will be possible when infrastructure improvements are complete. Initially however only eight-car Class 465 trains are in service, usually both sets being to the same specification. A pair of Class 465/2 units is seen forming a Hayes–Charing Cross service in February 1993. *Brian Morrison*

The Networker interiors benefit from air conditioning, but only the ABB Class 465/0 gives the passenger some direct control. Note the adjustable ventilation nozzles between luggage racks and windows. The Networkers are 'five-star' comfort compared with the dirty, grimy 40-year old EPBs they replace. *Brian Morrison*

Above A two-car unit of 466 stock outside Gillingham servicing depot prior to the Class's entry into service on Kent Link branch line work in spring 1993.
Brian Morrison

Left BR design 2-EPB Class 416/2 units Nos.6273/75 lead a Class 415/4 on a Victoria–Orpington service
Brian Morrison

At Waterloo East refurbished Class 416/4 unit No.6402 leads three Class 416/2 units on empty stock from Charing Cross to Slade Green depot for servicing.
Brian Morrison

Three-car 'Oxted' Class 207 Diesel Electric Multiple Unit No.207017 seen on a Reading–Salisbury service at Basingstoke on 23rd May 1992. *Dave Titheridge*

Refurbished Class 421/4 units 1832/33 make a rare appearance on the Hampton Court branch with a flower show special train for Waterloo. The flower show was an NSE sponsored event. *Brian Morrison*

Fast acceleration with revised gearing and a slightly higher speed are possible with the Class 421/5 'Greyhound' units, primarily used on the Waterloo–Portsmouth routes. The 22 units are maintained at Eastleigh depot. Unit No.1321 is seen at Portchester in March 1992 on a Portsmouth Harbour–Eastleigh–Waterloo service. *Dave Titheridge*

Wessex Electric units now include duties on the Waterloo–Portsmouth line. No.2401 is seen passing Clapham Junction on 31st July 1992 whilst Class 423/0 No.3093 passes on a Victoria–Horsham service. *Brian Morrison*

A Class 455/7 unit forming a Hampton Court–Waterloo service passes New Malden in January 1992. Note the third coach has a lower roof profile having previously been part of Class 508 units, now on Regional Railways North West Wirral services.
Brian Morrison

Two Class 438 4TC units have been restored for Charter Unit use. Nos.410/17 are seen leaving Blackfriars en-route to Sevenoaks. They are maintained on the South Western division at Bournemouth. *Brian Morrison*

Interior of Class 438 (4TC) coach on charter work. *Brian Morrison*

A four-car Class 415 4-EPB unit numbered 5001 has been formed in the original style complete with closed compartment trailer coaches. The unit is repainted in the original malachite green and used for special duties. However, poor condition of other Class 415 units and delays in accepting new Class 465 units have led to its continued use occasionally in normal service. In this view it is seen at Willesborough Crossing, Ashford, on a special shuttle service to Folkestone Harbour. *Brian Morrison*

A summer Saturday service, the 10.47 Basingstoke–Paignton via Southampton, Salisbury and Exeter, provided a pair of Class 47 locomotives, 47423 and 47701, for power when seen at Eastleigh on 20th June 1992. *Dave Titheridge*

The Isle of Wight has nine 'new' two-car Class 483 EMUs refurbished by BRML Eastleigh from 1938 London Underground tube stock. Two units are seen at Ryde St John's Road.
R.J. Greenaway

A car of the new Class 482 Waterloo & City line stock shortly after delivery from ABB in March 1993. Commissioning of the trains was undertaken at London Underground's Ruislip depot, where similar stock for the Central line is in course of delivery.
Brian Morrison

Approaching the end of their life as we went to press were the 1940 built Class 487 units on the Waterloo & City line. Motor coach No.56 is seen at Bank at the rear of a five-car train for Waterloo in June 1991.
Brian Morrison

CHANNEL TUNNEL TRAINS

European Passenger Services Ltd (EPSL) and Railfreight Distribution's European Division (RfD) are purchasing pathways from Eurotunnel through the Channel tunnel for operation of their trains. The EPSL trains will be marketed as the Eurostar service, initially from London Waterloo to Paris Gare du Nord and Bruxelles Midi. SNCF has also constructed new stations at Fréthun, for the Pas de Calais area, and Lille, dedicated to international services. BR's Union Railways arm, responsible for new route infrastructure, is proposing a station at Ashford, Kent.

The 31 Capitals express trains will all be formed of two identical half-sets with articulated bogies on all vehicles including the driving motor coach, thus normally allowing division at one of the three maintenance depots (one for each city) at the half-set point. EPSL will own 11, SNCF (France) 16 and SNCB (Belgium) four sets although operationally the customer should not detect any differences. Ten passenger coaches on each full set will be Second Class (584 seats), six First Class (210 seats) and two will be bar and buffet vehicles. Standing customers will not be allowed.

Later, seven north of London day-trains, all EPSL-owned, will be introduced to Birmingham, Manchester and Edinburgh but these are having to be limited to eight Standard Class (464 seats) and four First Class (114 seats) coaches plus two bar and buffet vehicles. The longer trains will not be operated north of London in the foreseeable future due to signalling equipment and station platform lengths.

The Chancellor of the Exchequer announced in his 1993 budget agreement in principle for proceeding with the new fast line from London to Folkestone, saving a further 30 minutes on journey times.

Within the giant North Pole (Acton) depot complex virtually any repair will be possible and facilities exist to check the three different current supply systems (25kv AC in the tunnel and on SNCF plus BR's East and West Coast routes and the new line, 750v DC on NSE (South) lines from Waterloo to Folkestone, 3000v DC on SNCB lines) and the variations in signalling controls transmitted by radio signals to the trains. The trains' construction is led by GEC Alsthom, mainly concentrated at Belfort, south-west France, with some vehicles fitted out at their Metro-Cammell works, Washwood Heath, Birmingham.

Night Sleeper trains are also planned from Glasgow, Plymouth and Swansea to Paris and Brussels, whilst London trains will serve Amsterdam, Köln, Dortmund and Frankfurt. European Night Services (ENS) will have 139 coaches for these services which it is hoped to introduce in 1995. On electrified routes in Britain seven new Class 92 locomotives, built by Brush Traction, from a fleet of 46 owned by Railfreight Distribution and SNCF will haul trains throughout and to at least Fréthun in France, but elsewhere BR diesel traction, tentatively pairs of InterCity owned Class 37s plus a generator van, will be required to and from London.

The trains have been designed for a 30-year life with British investment of £608 million in traction and rolling stock. A maintenance cycle calls for a total exam (Grande Visite Général) lasting about a week at 18-monthly intervals, a major overhaul at approximately eight years, including repaint, and a complete refurbishment (Operation de Confort Esthétique) at 15 years. On-board diagnostic monitoring equipment on all trains supplies data to the maintenance depots at North Pole, Le Lundy (Paris) and Forest (Bruxelles); this can be interrogated at any time to allow the depot to prepare for the train's arrival and effect necessary attention in the minimum time or exchange the set before its next booked duty. Trains must not enter the tunnel without both power cars or two locomotives working.

A power car of the new Class 373 Eurostar trains which will initially operate between London Waterloo International, Paris and Brussels through the Channel Tunnel in mid-1994. The coach interior views below provide a comparison of First and Second Class seating. *EPSL*

LOCOMOTIVES - PASSENGER SERVICE FLEET

INTERCITY

DIESEL CLASSES 37/0, 37/4* & 37/5†
Owning businesses: Railfreight Distribution *
West Coast (Scotland)
Built: English Electric 1962-65
Number series: 37059-37285, 37401-24*,
37510† **Fleet size:** 13, 3 of 8*, 1†
Main depots: Inverness, Motherwell*
Engine: English Electric 12CVST, 1,750hp
Traction motors: Six EE538A
Main generator/alternator*†: EE Type
822/10G, Brush BA100SA*†
Length: 61.5ft
Weight: 103-108 tonnes
Wheel arrangement: Co-Co
Maximum speed: 80mph
Fuel capacity: Classes 37/4, 37/5 and 7
Class 37/0: 1,690 gall; others 890 gall.
ETH Index: 30*
Notes: Classes 37/0 and 37/5 are for sleeper
services (with generator van for heating) and
infrastructure trains. Many are owned by RfD
but on hire to InterCity. RfD has to have any
three of eight Class 37/4s for InterCity West
Highland line and Charter use.

DIESEL CLASS 43

Owning businesses: East Coast main line
(IEC), Great Western main line (IWR),
Cross Country (ICC), Midland main line
(IML) and West Coast main line (IWC).
Built: BREL Crewe 1976-82
Number series: 43002-43198
Fleet size: IEC: 22, IWR: 88, ICC: 50;
IML: 31; IWC: 6
Main depots: Neville Hill (Leeds), St Philips
Marsh (Bristol), Laira (Plymouth),
Craigentinny (Edinburgh)
Engine: Paxman Valenta 12RP200L,
2,250hp, or Mirrlees Blackstone
MP190 2,250hp
Traction motors: Four Brush TMH68-46 or
GEZ417AZ
Main alternator: Brush BA1001B
Length: 58.4ft (59.9ft if buffers fitted)
Weight: 70t **Wheel arrangement:** Bo-Bo
Maximum speed: 125mph
Fuel capacity: 1,000 gall **ETH Index:** 66
Notes: Single driving cab, for operation only
as part of IC125 (High Speed Train) set.
Normally at front and rear of train. Movements
between depots possible 'Back to Back', or as

single units with cab leading. See also
Coaching Stock section.
Eight modified in 1988 for push-pull use with
Class 91 locomotives on East Coast main line
at 125mph before introduction of Mk4 coaches.

DIESEL CLASS 47/4

Owning businesses: Midland and Cross
Country (ICC) and Charter (ICH).
Built: British Railways, Crewe and Brush
Engineering Ltd 1962-67
Number series: 47805-53
Fleet size: ICC: 36, ICH: 8
Main depot: Bristol Bath Road
Engine: Sulzer 12LDA28C, 2,580hp
Traction motors: Six Brush TM64-68 Mk1A
Main generator: Brush TG172-50 Mk1
Length: 63.5ft **Weight:** 123t
Wheel arrangement: Bo-Bo
Maximum speed: 95mph
Fuel capacity: 1,220 gall **ETH Index:** 66

ELECTRO-DIESEL CLASS 73/2

Owning business: InterCity Gatwick Express
Built: 1965-67
Number series: 73201-35 **Fleet size:** 12
Main depot: Battersea Stewarts Lane
(London)
Traction motors: Four English Electric
EE542A
Power supply: Diesel engine: English
Electric 4SRKT Mk2, 600hp
Main generator: English Electric
EE824/5D
Electric: Third rail 600-750v dc,
1,420hp.
Diesel fuel capacity: 310 gall
ETH Index: 66.
Note: Modified version of Class 73/1 with flash
guards. Regularly used in Push-Pull modes.

Photo: Brian Morrison

ELECTRIC CLASSES 86/1 & 86/2*:
Owning businesses: West Coast main line
(IWC), Cross Country (ICC) and
Anglia (IAN)
Built: British Railways, Crewe, and English
Electric 1965-66
Number series: 86101-03, 86204-61*
Fleet size: IWC: 25, ICC: 17, IAN: 13.
Main depots: Willesden (London), Longsight
(Manchester) and Norwich.
Traction motors/Performance: *86/1:* Four
GEC type G412 AZ; 5,000hp
86/2: Four AEI type 282 AZ; 4,040hp
Length: 58.5ft   **Weight:** 86t
Wheel arrangement: Bo-Bo
Maximum speed: *86/1:* 110mph;
86/2: 100mph
ETH Index: 95 (600 amps-Mk2 d/e/f & Mk3
stock); 66 (400 amps- pre-Mk2 d stock)

ELECTRIC CLASS 87/0
Owning business: West Coast main line
(IWC)
Built: BREL Crewe 1973-74
Number series: 87001-35   **Fleet size:** 35
Main depot: Willesden (London)
Traction motors/Performance: Four GEC
type G412 AZ; 5,000hp
Length: 58.5ft   **Weight:** 83.3t
Wheel arrangement: Bo-Bo
Maximum speed: 110mph
ETH Index: 95 (600 amps – Mk2 d/e/f & Mk3
stock); 66 (400 amps – pre-Mk2 d stock)

ELECTRIC CLASS 90/0
Owning business: West Coast main line
(IWC)
Built: BREL Crewe 1988
Number series: 90001-15   **Fleet size:** 15
Main depot: Willesden (London)
Traction motors/Performance: Four GEC
type G412 BZ; 4,850hp
Length: 61.5ft   **Weight:** 84.5t
Wheel arrangement: Bo-Bo
Maximum speed: 110mph
ETH Index: 95 (600 amps – Mk2 d/e/f, Mks 3
& 4 stock); 66 (400 amps – pre-Mk2 d stock)
Note: RfD owned Nos 90022-25 are available
for loan to InterCity, usually on East Coast
route weekend Charter duties until the
opening of the Channel Tunnel.

ELECTRIC CLASS 91
Owning business: East Coast main line
(IEC)
Built: BREL Crewe for GEC 1988-91
Number series: 91001-31   **Fleet size:** 31
Main depot: Bounds Green (London)
Traction motors/Performance: Four GEC
G426, 6,350 hp
Length: 63.7t   **Weight:** 84.1t
Wheel arrangement: Bo-Bo
Maximum speed: 140mph (100mph if driven
from No.2 end)
ETH Index: 95 (600 amps – Mk2 d/e/f, Mks 3
& 4 stock); 66 (400 amps – pre-Mk2 d stock)

REGIONAL RAILWAYS

DIESEL CLASSES 31/1 & 31/4*
Owning businesses: North West*, Central
(all in joint ownership with infrastructure)
Built: Brush Traction 1959-61
Number series: 31146-66 (summer duties),
31408-65*
Fleet size: 3, 13*
Main depots: Bescot, Crewe*
Engine: English Electric 12SVT, 1,470hp
Traction motors: Four Brush TM73-68
Main generator: Brush TG160-48
Length: 56.8ft   **Weight:** 109 tonnes
Wheel arrangement: A1A-A1A
Maximum speed: 75mph, 90mph*
Fuel capacity: 530 gall
ETH Index: 66*

DIESEL CLASSES 37/0, 37/3* & 37/4†
Owning businesses: ScotRail, North West
(including Infrastructure)
Built: English Electric 1960-65
Number series: 37025-37294, 37351*,
37402-29†
Fleet size: 18, 1*, 4†
Main depots: Inverness, Crewe diesel
Engine: English Electric 12CVST, 1,750hp
Traction motors: Six EE538A
Main generator/alternator†: English Electric
Type 822/10G; Brush BA100SA†
Length: 61.5ft   **Weight:** 103-108 tonnes
Wheel arrangement: Co-Co
Maximum speed: 80mph
Fuel capacity: 890 gall (ten Cl.37/0 only), all
others 1,690 gall
ETH Index: 30†

NETWORK SOUTHEAST

DIESEL CLASSES 33/0 & 33/1*

Owning business: West of England (stand-by and special duties)
Built: Birmingham Railway Carriage and Wagon 1960-61
Numbered: 33035, 33114*   **Fleet size:** 1, 1*
Main depot: Eastleigh
Engine: Sulzer 8LDA28, 1,550hp
Traction motors: Four Crompton Parkinson C171C2
Main generator: Crompton Parkinson CG391B1
Length: 50.8ft   **Weight:** 78t
Wheel arrangement: Bo-Bo
Maximum speed: 85mph
Fuel capacity: 750 gall   **ETH Index:** 48
Notes: Some other Class 33 locomotives owned by NSE infrastructure may be borrowed in emergency. Most are restricted to 60mph and do not have operational train heating equipment. Class 33/1 are fitted with Push-Pull equipment and are able to be controlled by some designs of multiple unit including the Class 438 Charter trains.

DIESEL CLASSES 47/4 & 47/7*

Owning business: West of England
Built: British Railways, Crewe and Brush Engineering Ltd 1964-67
Number series: 47579-83, 47701-17*,
Fleet size: 2, 15*
Main depot: Old Oak Common (London)
Engine: Sulzer 12LDA28C, 2,580hp
Traction motors: Six Brush TM64-68 Mk1A
Main generator: Brush TG172-50 Mk1
Length: 63.5ft   **Weight:** 120t*, 123t
Wheel arrangement: Bo-Bo
Maximum speed: 95mph, 100mph*
Fuel capacity: 720 gall, 1,295 gall*
ETH Index: 66
Notes: Many of the locomotives are on loan from Rail express systems. These are being displaced by new Class 159 DMUs between March and July 1993.

DIESEL CLASS 50

Owning business: Charter.
Built: English Electric 1967-68
Number series: 50007-50   **Fleet size:** 3
Main depot: Laira (Plymouth)
Engine: English Electric 16CSVT, 2,700hp
Traction motors: Six English Electric EE538/5A
Main generator: English Electric EE840/4B
Length: 68.5ft   **Weight:** 116.9t
Wheel arrangement: Co-Co
Maximum speed: 100mph
Fuel capacity: 1,055 gall
ETH Index: 61
Note: Not available for normal service use.

ELECTRO-DIESEL CLASS 73/1

Owning business: West of England (special duties)
Built: English Electric 1966
Numbered: 73109   **Fleet size:** 1
Main depot: Battersea Stewarts Lane (London)
Traction motors: Four English Electric EE546/1B
Power supply: Diesel engine: English Electric 4SRKT Mk2, 600hp
   Main generator: English Electric EE824/5D
   Electric: Third rail 600-750V dc, 1,420hp
Length: 53.7ft   **Weight:** 76.8t
Wheel arrangement: Bo-Bo
Maximum speed: 90mph
Diesel fuel capacity: 310 gall
ETH Index: 66 on electric power. Diesel main generator able to pre-heat only.
Note: NSE also owns other Class 73 locomotives for infrastructure duties. These are usually restricted to 60mph. Under special circumstances some can be used, including Pullman liveried No.73101.

HAULED PASSENGER COACHING STOCK
INTERCITY

MARK 1 STANDARD VEHICLES:
Built as indicated against vehicle types
Construction: Steel bodies, 20.45 metres
    long
Maximum speed: 100mph
Heating and ventilation: Electric. Droplight
    windows in doors and small sliding
    ventilation windows for each bay or
    compartment
Customer access: Three catch-lock doors on
    side of vehicle, except catering coaches
    which have two only, some for emergency
    use only. On VIP Charter trains the middle
    doors are locked out of use

RESTAURANT FIRST KITCHEN OPEN,
Mk.1, RFO, AJ1.06
Built: BR Ashford and Swindon 1961
Business: Charter
Numbered: 325   **Fleet size:** 1
ETH Index: 2   **Cooking:** Electric
Seats: 24

RESTAURANT BUFFET WITH KITCHEN,
Mk1, RBR, Codes AJ4.03, AJ4.16, AJ4.17,
AJ4.19
Built: Pressed Steel 1960-61
Businesses: Anglia (8), Charter (14)
Number series: 1645-99   **Fleet size:** 22
ETH Index: 2
Cooking: Electric or Liquid Gas
Seats: 21, 22 or 23 some with wheelchair
    facilities

RESTAURANT MINIATURE BUFFET, Mk1,
RMB, Codes AN2.03, AN2.08
Built: BR Wolverton 1960-62
Businesses: Cross Country & Midland (3),
    Charter (2)
Number series: 1832-71   **Fleet size:** 5
ETH Index: 3   **Cooking:** Liquid Gas
Seats: 44   **Toilets:** 2

SLEEPER STAFF COACH, Mk1, SLSC,
Code AU5.01
Built: BR Derby 1964, BCK converted at BR
    Cathays 1988
Business: Charter
Number series: 2833-34   **Fleet size:** 2
ETH Index: 3
Berths: Five twin-bed berths for staff only
Seats: Loose seating with small kitchen area
    for staff only
Toilet: 1

FIRST OPEN, Mk1, FO, Code AD1.03
Built: BRCW 1959*, BR Swindon 1962-63
Business: Charter
Number series: 3097-3100*, 3107-50
Fleet size: 3*, 22   **ETH Index:** 3
Seats: 42   **Toilets:** 2

TOURIST STANDARD OPEN, Mk1, TSO,
Code AC2.01
Built: BR Wolverton 1959-62
Business: Charter
Number series: 4842-5041
Fleet size: 27 (including two on loan to SRPS)
ETH Index: 4
Seats: 64   **Toilets:** 2

FIRST CORRIDOR, Mk1, FK, Code AA1.01
Built: BR Swindon 1962
Business: Charter
Numbered: 13318   **Fleet size:** 1
ETH Index: 3
Seats: 42   **Toilets:** 2

BRAKE FIRST CORRIDOR, Mk1, BFK, Code
AB1.01
Built: BR Swindon 1961-63
Business: Charter
Number series: 17015-23   **Fleet size:** 2
ETH Index: 2
Seats: 24   **Toilet:** 1

BRAKE COMPOSITE CORRIDOR, Mk1,
BCK, Codes AB3.01*, AB3.02
Built: BR Swindon 1962* and BR Derby 1964
Business: Charter
Number series: 21246*, 21266-74
Fleet size: 1*, 4   **ETH Index:** 3
Seats: 1st 12, Std 18*; 1st 12, Std 24
Toilets: 2

BRAKE STANDARD CORRIDOR, Mk1, BSK,
Code AB2.01
Built: BR Wolverton 1963
Business: Charter
Numbered: 35469   **Fleet size:** 1
ETH Index: 2
Seats: 24   **Toilet:** 1
Note: Includes a generator for train heating of
    steam hauled services.

MARK 2D, 2E & 2F STANDARD VEHICLES
Built: BR Derby
Construction: Steel bodies, 20.63 metres
    long

Maximum speed: 100mph
Heating and ventilation: Electric, air conditioning driven by locomotive or generator coach
Customer access: Wide catch-lock doors on side at each end of vehicle. Standard corridor connections on ends of all vehicles

FIRST OPEN, Mk2D, FO, Code AD1.05
Built: 1971
Businesses: Charter (7), Cross Country & Midland (1)
Number series: 3178-3202   **Fleet size:** 8
ETH Index: 5
Seats: 42   **Toilets:** 2

TOURIST STANDARD OPEN, Mk2D, TSO, Code AC2.09
Built: 1971
Businesses: Cross Country & Midland (48), Anglia (10), Charter (5)
Number series: 5616-5743   **Fleet size:** 63
ETH Index: 5
Seats: 64   **Toilets:** 2

STANDARD OPEN, Mk2D, SO, Code AC2.17
Built: 1971-72, converted at BREL Derby from FO 1989-90
Businesses: West Coast (17*), Cross Country & Midland (10), Great Western (4), Charter (5)
Number series: 6200-35   **Fleet size:** 36
ETH Index: 5   **Seats:** 58
Toilets: 2 (* Six ex-Stagecoach Rail each have only one)

RESTAURANT-MICRO BUFFET, Mk2D, RMBT, Code AN2.07
Built: 1971, conversion by BREL Derby from TSO(T) in 1985
Business: Cross Country & Midland
Number series: 6652-65   **Fleet size:** 5
ETH Index: 6
Seats: 47   **Toilet:** 1

BRAKE STANDARD OPEN, Mk2D, BSO, Code AE2.06
Built: 1971
Businesses: Cross Country & Midland(6), Great Western (3)
Number series: 9480-94   **Fleet size:** 9
ETH Index: 5
Seats: 31   **Toilet:** 1

FIRST CORRIDOR, Mk2D, FK, Code AA1.09
Built: 1971-72
Business: Charter
Number series: 13585-13607   **Fleet size:** 3
ETH Index: 5
Seats: 42   **Toilets:** 2

BRAKE FIRST CORRIDOR, Mk2D, BFK, Code AB1.06
Built: BR Derby 1971-72
Businesses: West Coast (2), Charter (14)
Number series: 17141-72   **Fleet size:** 16
ETH Index: 5
Seats: 24   **Toilet:** 1

FIRST OPEN, Mk2E, FO, Code AD1.06
Built: 1972-73
Businesses: West Coast (3), Cross Country & Midland (10), Anglia (5), Charter (24)
Number series: 3221-75   **Fleet size:** 42
ETH Index: 5   **Toilets:** 2
Seats: 42 or 41 with wheelchair facilities

FIRST OPEN (MICRO-BUFFET), Mk2E, FO(T), Code AG1.01
Built: 1971 as FO, converted BRML Springburn 1992 for Sleeper Lounge Car use.
Businesses: Great Western (3), Cross Country & Midland (3)
Number series: 3520-25   **Fleet size:** 6
ETH Index: 5
Seats: 36   **Toilets:** 2

TOURIST STANDARD OPEN, Mk2E, TSO, Code AC2.10
Built: 1972
Businesses: West Coast (3), Cross Country & Midland (83), Charter (10)
Number series: 5744-5907   **Fleet size:** 96
ETH Index: 5
Seats: 64   **Toilets:** 2

BRAKE STANDARD OPEN, Mk2E, BSO, Code AE2.07
Built: 1972
Businesses: Great Western (1), Cross Country & Midland (9)
Number series: 9496-9509   **Fleet size:** 10
ETH Index: 5
Seats: 32   **Toilet:** 1

RESTAURANT LOUNGE FIRST, Mk2F, RLF, Code AJ1.04
Built: 1973. Conversions in 1988 and 1991 from FO & SO fleets
Business: Cross Country & Midland
Number series: 1200-60   **Fleet size:** 32
ETH Index: 5
Seats: 26   **Toilets:** 2

FIRST OPEN, Mk2F, FO, Code AD1.07
Built: 1973
Businesses: West Coast (57), Anglia (21)
Number series: 3277-3438
Fleet size: 78
ETH Index: 5

Seats: 39 or 42   **Toilets:** 2

Note: Some vehicles have electrical adaptors to power Mk1 RFBs on Anglia services

TOURIST STANDARD OPEN, Mk2F, TSO, Codes AC2.11, AC2.15

Built: 1973-75

Businesses: West Coast (110), Cross Country & Midland (67), Anglia (26)

Number series: 5908-6184   **Fleet size:** 203

ETH Index: 5

Seats: 64 or 62 with wheelchair facilities

Toilets: 2 (some with facilities for disabled)

RESTAURANT LOUNGE BUFFET FIRST, Mk2F, Codes AN1.01*, AN1.02

Built: 1973-74, converted from FO at BR RTC* and BR Ilford Depot 1987 & 1989

Business: West Coast

Number series: 6700/01*, 6702-08

Fleet size: 9   **ETH Index:** 5*, 6

Seats: 26 loose lounge chairs   **Toilet:** 1

TOURIST STANDARD OPEN, Mk2F, TSO, Code AC2.24

Built: 1973-75 as FO. Converted to SO (42 seats) in 1985, reseated to present style by BREL Derby and RFS Industries, in 1990

Business: Anglia

Number series: 6800-29   **Fleet size:** 30

ETH Index: 5

Seats: 74   **Toilets:** 2

BRAKE STANDARD OPEN, Mk2F, BSO, Code AE2.08

Built: 1974

Business: Cross Country & Midland

Number series: 9513-39   **Fleet size:** 16

ETH Index: 5

Seats: 32   **Toilet:** 1

DRIVING BRAKE STANDARD OPEN, Mk2F, DBSO, Code AF2.01

Built: 1974, converted from BSO 1979-86

Business: Anglia

Number series: 9701-14   **Fleet size:** 13

ETH Index: 5

Seats: 32   **Toilet:** 1

MARK 3A & 3B STANDARD VEHICLES

Built: BR Derby

Construction: Steel bodies, 23 metres long

Maximum speed: 125mph

Heating and ventilation: Electric, air conditioning driven by locomotive or generator coach

Customer access: Wide catch-lock doors on side at each end of vehicle. Standard corridor connections on ends of all vehicles

RESTAURANT FIRST MODULAR Mk3A, RFM, Codes AJ1.01*, AJ1.03

Built: 1975-80. Conversions in 1984 from TRUK (IC125), FO & RFB designs

Businesses: West Coast (52), Anglia (6)

Number series: 10200/01*, 10202-60

Fleet size: 2*, 56   **ETH Index:** 16*, 14

Seats: 24*, 22   **Toilet:** 1 (staff)

SLEEPER WITH PANTRY Mk3A, SLEP, Code AU4.01

Built: 1981

Businesses: West Coast (50), Cross Country (15) Great Western (11), Charter (6)

Number series: 10500-10617

Fleet size: 82   **ETH Index:** 7

Berths: 12 compartments x 2 (single occupancy for 1st Class)

Toilets: 2

SLEEPER Mk3A, SLE, Code AS4.04

Built: 1981

Businesses: West Coast (48), Charter (10)

Number series: 10646-10732

Fleet size : 58   **ETH Index:** 6

Berths: 13 compartments x 2 (single occupancy for 1st Class)

Toilets: 2

FIRST OPEN Mk3A, FO, Code AD1.08

Built: 1975

Business: West Coast

Number series: 11005-60   **Fleet size:** 35

ETH Index: 6

Seats: 48   **Toilets:** 2

FIRST OPEN Mk3B, FO, Code AD1.10

Built: 1984

Business: West Coast

Number series: 11064-11101   **Fleet size:** 38

ETH Index: 6

Seats: 48   **Toilets:** 2

Note: Some vehicles dedicated to Pullman service

TOURIST STANDARD OPEN Mk3A, TSO, Codes AC2.13, AC2.16, AC2.25*:

Built: 1975, * conversions from CO 1990

Business: West Coast

Number series: 12004-12165, 12166-72*

Fleet size: 164   **ETH Index:** 6

Seats: 76 or 74 with wheelchair facilities.

Toilets: 2 (some with facilities for disabled)

BRAKE FIRST OPEN, Mk3B, BFO, Code AE1.01

Built: 1985   **Business:** West Coast

Number series: 17173-75   **Fleet size:** 3

ETH Index: 6

Seats: 36   **Toilet:** 1

DRIVING VAN TRAILER Mk3, DVT, Code NZ5.02

Built: BREL Derby 1988. For push-pull operation. Replaces Gangwayed Brake van for conveyance of Train Conductor(s), large luggage, bicycles, parcels and mails in secured areas.

Construction: Steel bodies, 18.83 metres long. Corridor connection on rear end of vehicle only.

Business: West Coast

Number series: 82101-52   **Fleet size:** 52

Weight: 43.7t   **ETH Index:** 6

Van load capacity: 8t

MARK 3 INTERCITY 125 (HST) VEHICLES

Built: BREL Derby.

Construction: Steel bodies, 23 metres long

Maximum speed: 125mph

Heating and ventilation: Electric, air conditioning driven by Class 43 locomotive or generator coach

Customer access: Wide catch-lock doors on side at each end of vehicle. Standard corridor connections on ends of all vehicles

TRAILER RESTAURANT FIRST BUFFET, Mk3, TRFB, Code GN1.01

Built: 1976

Business: Great Western (11), Cross Country (4)

Number series: 40204-33   **Fleet size:** 15

ETH Index: 6

Seats: 23   **Toilet:** 1 (staff)

TRAILER RESTAURANT STANDARD BUFFET, Mk3, TRFB, Code GK2.02

Built: 1976

Business: Cross Country

Number series: 40401-37   **Fleet size:** 22

ETH Index: 6

Seats: 35   **Toilets:** 1 (staff)

TRAILER RESTAURANT FIRST KITCHEN, Mk3, TRFK, Code GL1.01

Built: 1976

Businesses: East Coast (1), Midland (1), Great Western (1)

Number series: 40501-11   **Fleet size:** 3

ETH Index: 6

Seats: 24   **Toilets:** 1 (staff)

TRAILER LOUNGE UNCLASSIFIED WITH KITCHEN, Mk3, TLUK, Code GM4.01

Built: 1976, converted in 1984 from TRFK

Business: Cross Country (special duties)

Numbered: 40513   **Fleet size:** 1

ETH Index: 6

Seats: 16 (eight at conference table and eight loose chairs)   **Toilets:** 1 (staff)

TRAILER RESTAURANT FIRST MODULAR, Mk3, TRFM, Code GK1.02

Built: 1976, converted in 1987 from TRFB.

Business: Midland (Master Cutler Pullman)

Numbered: 40619   **Fleet size:** 1

ETH Index: 6

Seats: 17   **Toilets:** 1 (staff)

TRAILER RESTAURANT FIRST BUFFET, Mk3, TRFB, Code GK1.01

Built: 1976

Businesses: West Coast (3), East Coast (11), Great Western (29), Midland (14)

Number series: 40700-57   **Fleet size:** 57

ETH Index: 6

Seats: 17   **Toilets:** 1 (staff)

TRAILER FIRST, Mk3, TF, Code GH1.02

Built: 1976-82

Businesses: West Coast (6), East Coast (21), Great Western (79), Midland (32), Cross Country (25)

Number series: 41003-41178

Fleet size: 163

ETH Index: 6

Seats: 48 (47 when table and seat removed for wheelchair passengers)   **Toilets:** 2

TRAILER STANDARD, Mk3, TS, Codes GH2.03, GH2.04

Built: 1976-82

Businesses: West Coast (12), East Coast (41), Great Western (151), Midland (55), Cross Country (93)

Number series: 42003-42359   **Fleet size:** 352

ETH Index: 6

Seats: 76   **Toilets:** 2

TRAILER GUARD STANDARD, Mk3, TGS, Code GJ2.01

Built: 1976-82. Lockable secure compartment at one end of vehicle for Conductor Guard, including access to Class 43 locomotive (power car)

Businesses: West Coast (4), East Coast (11), Great Western (41), Midland (16), Cross Country (26)

Number series: 44000-44101   **Fleet size:** 98

ETH Index: 6

Seats: 61 - 63 and facilities for wheelchair passengers   **Toilet:** 1

MARK 4 STANDARD VEHICLES

Built: 1990-92

Main contractor: GEC Metro-Cammell, Washwood Heath, Birmingham

Construction: Extruded aluminium bodies, 23 metres long; DVT 18.59 metres long

Business: East Coast

Maximum speed: 140mph

Heating and ventilation: Electric, air conditioning driven by locomotive or generator coach

Customer access: Wide plug doors on side at each end of vehicle. Standard corridor connections on both ends of most vehicles, DVT and TSOE one end only.

SERVICE VEHICLE (RESTAURANT FIRST MODULAR), Mk4, SV, Code AJ1.05

Number series: 10300-33	**Fleet size:** 34
ETH Index: 6	**Seats:** 20

Toilets: 2 (one large with extra facilities)

PULLMAN (FIRST) OPEN, Mk4, PO, Code AD1.11

Number series: 11200-76	**Fleet size:** 69
ETH Index: 6	**Seats:** 46

Toilets: 2 (one large with extra facilities)

TOURIST STANDARD OPEN - END, Mk4, TSOE, Code AI2.01

Number series: 12200-32	**Fleet size:** 32
ETH Index: 6	**Seats:** 74

Toilets: 2 (one large with extra facilities)

TOURIST STANDARD OPEN - DISABLED, Mk4, TSOD, Code AL2.01

Number series: 12300-30	**Fleet size:** 31
ETH Index: 6	

Seats: 72 plus wheelchair facilities

Toilets: 1 large with special facilities for disabled

TOURIST STANDARD OPEN, Mk4, TSO, Code AC2.14

Number series: 12400-12538	**Fleet size:** 116
ETH Index: 6	**Seats:** 74

Toilets: 2 (one large with extra facilities)

DRIVING VAN TRAILER, Mk4, DVT, Code NZ5.01

Built: 1990-91 for push-pull operation and conveyance of Train Conductor(s), large luggage, bicycles, parcels and mails in secured areas.

Number series: 82200-31	**Fleet size:** 32
Weight: 43.5t	
ETH Index: 6	

Van load capacity: 8t

On 27th July 1991, the 08.00 King's Cross–Edinburgh service heads up Holloway Bank out of King's Cross with the unusual sight of a Mk4 DVT leading in this direction. The train had been turned round on a diversion caused by engineering works. It was powered at the rear by Class 91 No.91002.
Brian Morrison

TOURIST STANDARD OPEN, Mk1, SO, Code AC2.01
Built: BR Wolverton 1959-62
Businesses: *Regional Railways:* North West (5a), Central (9v, 1a) *Network SouthEast:* Thames (1v)
Number series: 3769-5001
Fleet size: RR:15, NSE: 1   **ETH Index:** 4
Brakes: Vacuum (v)* or Air (a)
Seats: 48   **Toilets:** 2
Note: * Retained for special duties only, including steam haulage

FIRST CORRIDOR, Mk1, FK, Code AA1.01
Built: BR Swindon 1962
Business: *Regional Railways:* North West (1), Central (1)
Number series: 13225-27   **Fleet size:** 2
ETH Index: 3   **Brakes:** Dual
Seats: 42   **Toilets:** 2

BRAKE STANDARD CORRIDOR, Mk1, BSK, Code AB2.01
Built: BR Wolverton 1962-63
Businesses: *Regional Railways:* Central (2)
Numbered: 35452/53
Fleet sizes: RR: 2
ETH Index: 2   **Brakes:** Vacuum
Seats: 24   **Toilet:**1
Note: Retained for special duties only, including steam haulage

MARK 2, 2A, 2B & 2C VEHICLES
Built: BR Derby 1965-69
Construction: Steel bodies, catch-lock doors on side at each end and centre of vehicle. Standard corridor connections on ends of all vehicles
Length: Mk2, Mk2A: 20.45 metres, Mk2B, Mk2C: 20.63 metres
Maximum speed: 100mph
Heating and ventilation: Electric, driven by locomotive or generator coach

TOURIST STANDARD OPEN, Mk2, TSO, Code AC2.0
Businesses: *Regional Railways:* ScotRail (46) Central (1) *Network SouthEast:* Thames (1)
Number series: 5085-5226
Fleet size: RR: 47 (seven in Hebridean Heritage livery), NSE: 1 (for steam hauled special services)
ETH Index: 4   **Brakes:** Vacuum
Seats: 64   **Toilets:** 2

STANDARD OPEN, Mk2, SO, Code AD2.03
Businesses: *Regional Railways:* ScotRail *Network SouthEast:* West of England
Number series: 5230-55
Fleet size: RR: 4 (two in Hebridean Heritage livery), NSE: 1
ETH Index: 4   **Brakes:** Vacuum
Seats: 48   **Toilets:** 2

BRAKE MICRO BUFFET, Mk2, BSO(T), Codes AH2.03, AH2.04*
Built: 1966 as BSO, converted 1983/86
Business: *Regional Railways:* ScotRail
Numbered: 9100/01, 9105*   **Fleet size:** 3
ETH Index: 4   **Brakes:** Vacuum
Seats: 27*, 31
Toilet: 1

BRAKE STANDARD OPEN, Mk2, BSO, Code AE2.03
Businesses: *Regional Railways:* ScotRail (3), *Network SouthEast:* Thames(2)
Number series: 9384-9414
Fleet size: RR: 3 (three in Hebridean Heritage livery), NSE: 2
ETH Index: 4   **Brakes:** Vacuum
Seats: 31   **Toilet:** 1

BRAKE FIRST CORRIDOR, Mk2, BFK, Code AB1.02
Business: *Regional Railways:* ScotRail
Numbered: 17039   **Fleet size:** 1
ETH Index: 4   **Brakes:** Vacuum
Seats: 24   **Toilet:** 1

TOURIST STANDARD OPEN, Mk2A, TSO, Code AC2.06
Businesses: *Regional Railways:* North West (18), Central (12), *Network SouthEast:* West of England (36)
Number series: 5259-5433
Fleet size: RR: 30, NSE: 36
ETH Index: 4   **Brakes:** Air
Seats: 64   **Toilets:** 2

BRAKE STANDARD OPEN, Mk2A, BSO, Code AE2.04
Businesses: *Regional Railways:* North West (5), Central (3)
Number series: 9417-38   **Fleet size:** 8
ETH Index: 4   **Brakes:** Air
Seats: 31   **Toilet:** 1

FIRST CORRIDOR, Mk2A, FK, Code AA1.06
Business: *Network SouthEast:* West of England
Number series: 13459-73   **Fleet size:** 4
ETH Index: 4   **Brakes:** Air
Seats: 42   **Toilets:** 2

BRAKE FIRST CORRIDOR, Mk2A, BFK, Code AB1.03
Businesses: *Regional Railways:* ScotRail (6)*
Network SouthEast: West of England (16)
Number series: 17056-99
Fleet size: RR: 6, NSE: 16
ETH Index: 4   **Brakes:** Vacuum* or Air
Seats: 24   **Toilet:** 1

BRAKE STANDARD CORRIDOR, Mk2A, BSK, Code AB2.04
Built: 1968 as BFK
Businesses: *Regional Railways:*
North West (1), Central (1)*
Numbered: 35500*, 35510   **Fleet size:** 2
ETH Index: 4   **Brakes:** Vacuum* or Air
Seats: 24   **Toilet:** 1

TOURIST STANDARD OPEN, Mk2B, TSO, Code AC2.07
Businesses: *Regional Railways:* North East (3), North West (1), Central (1), *Network SouthEast:* West of England (29)
Number series: 5435-97
Fleet size: RR: 5. NSE: 29
ETH Index: 4   **Brakes:** Air
Seats: 62   **Toilets:** 2

FIRST CORRIDOR, Mk2B, FK, Code AA1.07
Business: *Network SouthEast:* West of England
Number series: 13479-13507   **Fleet size:** 5
ETH Index: 4   **Brakes:** Air
Seats: 42   **Toilets:** 2

TOURIST STANDARD OPEN, Mk2C, TSO, Code AC2.08
Businesses: *Regional Railways:*
North West (2), Central (3)
Number series: 5505-5614   **Fleet size:** 5
ETH Index: 4   **Brakes:** Air
Seats: 62   **Toilets:** 2

MICRO-BUFFET STANDARD OPEN, Mk2C, TSO(T), Code AG2.01
Built: 1969, converted 1980
Business: *Regional Railways:* North East (2)
Network SouthEast: West of England (4)
Number series: 6500-28
Fleet size: RR: 2, NSE: 4
ETH Index: 4   **Brakes:** Air
Seats: 55   **Toilets:** 1

BRAKE STANDARD OPEN, Mk2C, BSO, Code AE2.05
Built: 1970
Businesses: *Regional Railways:*
North East (2), North West (1)
Number series: 9440-58   **Fleet size:** 3
ETH Index: 4   **Brakes:** Air
Seats: 31   **Toilet:** 1

FIRST CORRIDOR, Mk2C, FK, Code AA1.08
Business: *Network SouthEast:*
West of England
Numbered: 13525   **Fleet size:** 1
ETH Index: 4   **Brakes:** Air
Seats: 42   **Toilets:** 2

BRAKE FIRST CORRIDOR, Mk2C, BFK, Code AB1.05
Business: *Regional Railways:* North West (1)
Network SouthEast: West of England (5)
Number series: 17115-33
Fleet size: RR: 1, NSE 5
ETH Index: 4   **Brakes:** Air
Seats: 24   **Toilets:** 1

FIRST CORRIDOR, Mk2D, FK, Code AA1.09
For specification refer to InterCity section.
Business: *Network SouthEast:*
West of England
Numbered: 13575   **Fleet size:** 1

SPECIAL COACH
OBSERVATION CAR, SALOON, Code AD4.01
Built: Metro-Cammell 1958 as Class 101 DMU driving trailer
Construction: Steel body, 18.49 metres long
Maximum speed: 70mph   **Heating:** None
Business: *Regional Railways:* ScotRail
Numbered: 6300   **Fleet size:** 1
Seats: 42 (unclassified)   **Toilet:** 1

DIESEL MULTIPLE UNITS

REGIONAL RAILWAYS

ScotRail, North West and Central Divisions own various vehicles which have almost reached life expiry. Introduction of Class 323 EMUs on Birmingham Cross-City services early in 1993, modification of the final few Class 153 single car DMUs, rectification of design faults on Class 158s and refurbishment of selected Classes 101 and 117 DMUs will eliminate all other first generation designs. All first generation units have a maximum speed of 70mph and all motor vehicles have two Leyland 150hp engines unless otherwise shown. All Regional Railways stock, apart from ScotRail Class 158s, operates as Standard Class only although some retain seating to the higher specification. This publication is concerned solely with classifications for current operating practices.

CLASS 101

Built: Metropolitan-Cammell 1956-59.
Gangwayed within units.

DRIVING MOTOR BRAKE STANDARD, DMBS, Codes DQ2.02, DQ2.32*
Businesses: ScotRail (12), North West (23), Central (18), S.Wales & West (2)
Number series: 51175-51224, 51226*, 51228-53, 51426-63, 51800, 53164-65, 53198-53231, 53253-56, 53291-53315
Fleet size: 54, 1*   **Seats:** 49*, 52

DRIVING MOTOR STANDARD, DMSL, Codes DP2.10*, DP2.13†., DP2.14≠, DP2.-§
Businesses: ScotRail (10), North West (6), Central (11), S.Wales & West (2)
Number series: 51496*, 51499§, 51500*, 51501§, 51505-33*, 51803-08*, 53160-63≠, 53168-93≠, 53245†, 53266-69*, 53321-30*, 53333§, 53746*
Fleet sizes 18*, 7≠, 1†, 3§
Seats: 65*≠, 52†, 58§   **Toilet:** 1

DRIVING TRAILER STANDARD, DTSL, Codes DS2.06, DS2.11
Built: 1957-58
Businesses: North West (13), Central (11)
Number series: 54050-91, 54220, 54343-54408
Fleet size: 24
Seats: 65   **Toilet:** 1
TRAILER STANDARD, TSL, Codes DT2.02*, DT2.20, DT2.28†.

Business: ScotRail
Number series: 59111†, 59118, 59302-03*, 59536-39, 59570†
Fleet size: 2*, 3, 2†
Seats: 58†, 65, 71*   **Toilet:** 1

CLASS 108

Built: BR Derby 1958-60.
Gangwayed within units

DRIVING MOTOR BRAKE STANDARD, DMBS, Codes DQ2.12*, DQ2.13
Businesses: North West (4), Central (3)
Number series: 51907-47, 53627*, 53971*
Fleet size: 5, 2*   **Seats:** 52

DRIVING MOTOR STANDARD, DMSL, Codes DP2.19*, DP2.26, DP2.27†.
Businesses: North West (2), Central (5)
Number series: 51567/68, 52044-54†, 53632-45*
Fleet size: 2, 3†, 2*
Seats: 62*, 64, 65†   **Toilet:** 1

DRIVING TRAILER STANDARD, DTSL, Code DS2.07
Business: North West
Number series: 54203-08, 54256-70, 54490, 54504
Fleet size: 6
Seats: 65   **Toilet:** 1

CLASS 115

Built: BR Derby 1960. Constructed non-gangwayed; gangways subsequently fitted to all retained vehicles.
Engines: Two Leyland Albion 230bhp

DRIVING MOTOR BRAKE STANDARD, DMBS, Code DQ2.33
Business: Central
Number series: 51851-97
Fleet size: 11   **Seats:** 74

CLASSES 115 & 127

TRAILER STANDARD, TS, TSL*§Codes DT2.26§, DT2.27†., DT2.29≠, DT2.-§
Built: BR Derby 1959-60 to same specification. Constructed non-gangwayed, gangways subsequently fitted to all remaining vehicles
Business: Central
Number series: 59591-59614*, 59641-58≠, 59713≠, 59734-35≠, 59751†, 59753§
Fleet sizes: 10*, 1†, 5≠, 1§
Seats: 66§, 70†, 86*, 98≠   **Toilets:** 2*§

CLASS 116

Built: BR Derby, 1957-58. Constructed non-gangwayed, gangways subsequently fitted to all remaining vehicles

DRIVING MOTOR BRAKE STANDARD, DMBS, Code DQ2.30
Businesses: Central (13), South Wales & West (2)
Number series: 51128-40, 53053-90, 53818-63
Fleet size: 15   **Seats:** 65

DRIVING MOTOR STANDARD, DMS, Code DP2.20
Businesses: Central (15), South Wales & West (2)
Number series: 51141-51, 53101-32, 53897-53921
Fleet size: 17   **Seats:** 89

TRAILER STANDARD, TS, Codes DT2.09*, DT2.19
Business: Central
Numbered: 59032*, 59335, 59446
Fleet size: 1*, 2   **Seats:** 88, 98*

CLASS 117

Built: Pressed Steel 1959, Gangwayed within units.
Business: Central

DRIVING MOTOR BRAKE STANDARD, DMBS, Code DQ2.20
Number series: 51334-73
Fleet size: 14   **Seats:** 65

DRIVING MOTOR STANDARD, DMS, Code DP2.21
Number series: 51376-51415
Fleet size: 14   **Seats:** 89

TRAILER STANDARD, TSL, Codes DT2.-
Number series: 59486-59522
Fleet size: 14
Seats: 70   **Toilets:** 2

CLASS 118

Built: Birmingham RC&W Co 1960, Gangwayed within units.
Business: Central

DRIVING MOTOR BRAKE STANDARD, DMBS, Code DQ2.20
Number series: 51314-16
Fleet size: 2   **Seats:** 65

DRIVING MOTOR STANDARD, DMS, Code DP2.21
Number series: 51329-31
Fleet size: 2   **Seats:** 89

TRAILER STANDARD, TSL, Code DT2.30
Number series: 59481-83   **Fleet size:** 2
Seats: 70   **Toilets:** 2

CLASS 119

Built: Gloucester RC&W 1958
Business: Central

DRIVING MOTOR BRAKE STANDARD, DMBS, Code DQ2.—
Numbered: 51060
Fleet size: 1   **Seats:** 34

DRIVING MOTOR STANDARD, DMSL, Code DP2.03
Numbered: 51088   **Fleet size:** 1
Seats: 68   **Toilets:** 2

TRAILER STANDARD, TSL, Code DT2.16
Numbered: 59419   **Fleet size:** 1
Seats: 60   **Toilets:** 2

CLASS 122

DRIVING MOTOR BRAKE STANDARD, DMBS, Code DX2.02
Built: Gloucester RC&W 1958. Single cars, driving cab each end, non-gangwayed
Business: S. Wales & West
Number series: 55000-12
Fleet size: 5   **Seats:** 65

SECOND GENERATION UNITS

In 1981 BR took delivery of the first of a new type of diesel multiple unit. The prototype Class 140 two-car unit was a fixed wheelbase vehicle constructed by BR Derby Works using a Leyland bus body. The aim was to produce a new lightweight design vehicle for use on lightly used country routes and high capacity for urban commuter routes where electrification was not at that time viable. This led to a production fleet of 20 units for West Yorkshire, Leeds area, services (Class 141) and subsequently the rest of the Class 14x series. After a very poor early record, gearboxes were changed and a different braking system installed. Target availability is now 80%, whilst a further safety modification is being fitted to all 14x series units. In November 1992 a programme commenced to fit a Cummins LT10R 225hp engine to 100 Pacer vehicles as the Leyland TL11 is no longer produced. Initially the South Wales and West Class 143s and 25 units of North West Class 142s will be so fitted.

Undoubtedly the saviour of many Regional Railways routes has been the Sprinter. In 1984 two Class 150 prototype three-car units were built at BREL York, all vehicles motored. The following year two similar general specification units, Class 151, appeared from Metro-Cammell, Birmingham. Various engines and gearboxes have been tried on these and the production series of 135 Class 150 two-car units have been eminently successful in the reduction of costs and growth in traffic on routes which in many cases will never be self-financing. Cummins engines and Voith gearboxes have proved to be very reliable and their range of operation is extensive. The mechanics of the Class 151 were not standard to the other designs and regrettably BR did not place further orders to that specification with Metro-Cammell, therefore the units have been mothballed whilst a decision is made on what new use will be made of these either as one, two or three car units for passenger traffic or as future development equipment test trains based on the Railway Technical Centre, Derby.

Following the success of the first series Sprinters an improved saloon specification was required for longer distance routes in an attempt to eliminate high cost locomotive haulage of cascaded former InterCity hauled coaches. Thus orders were placed with two companies, Leyland Bus and Metro-Cammell, for the Classes 155 and 156. Sadly the former were initially very unreliable, particularly their plug fitting doors used for the first time in a production series train for BR. This was the first time Leyland Bus had gone into complete production of a train although the group had provided many excellent engines over many years and, as stated above, supplied bodies for many of the Pacer trains. On the other hand the Metro-Cammell Class 156 has been even more successful than the earlier Sprinters, and achieved constant 90%+ availability, adopting the sliding door, not plug fitting, design. Problems with the Class 155s and subsequently with the Class 158 (see below) led to much reorganisation of the then Provincial Sector business plans and extremely high planned usage was called for from Class 156s. For some months with 285hp per 38 ton coach they were very successfully drafted on to Edinburgh–Glasgow via Falkirk High services where they were being run up to 18 hours daily to run 40 miles in 46 minutes with two stops at a maximum of 75mph, timings designed for 2,500hp locomotives hauling seven coaches, 230 tons, to be taken over by the Class 158 designed for 90mph operation with 350hp per 38 ton coach.

In 1990 BR decided that many routes required a single car unit with a driving compartment each end, an updated version of the 1960s Class 121 and 122 cars. The specification called for a single engined 285hp unit for use on branch and very rural services which could also operate in multiple with each other and all designs of Pacer and Sprinter on branches and main lines at 75mph at times of higher demand. For this purpose the 35 BR owned two-car Class 155 units were taken to Hunslet-Barclay, Kilmarnock for conversion to single cars, classified Class 153. The Class 155s had worked long distance services from South Wales and were replaced by the Class 158. At this time West Yorkshire PTE lease seven Class 155s which do not feature in the conversion programme.

The success of the Sprinters can be gauged on the proposed introduction of 50 new trains, Class 157, which were subject to tender appraisal at the time of writing. Half of these are planned for expanded services for Strathclyde PTE (Glasgow area) and six each for the reopening of two East Midlands lines; of the remainder West Yorkshire PTE have expressed interest.

The Class 158 is Regional Railways (formerly Provincial) top of the range unit for 'Express' cross country services outwith the InterCity network. The train had several years bad publicity following its launch in 1989. The unit had a significant number of major design faults, partly because it was the first time this length of extruded aluminium body had been constructed in this country, and there were problems with the first four bodies which were produced overseas. Lack of such experience in design and production combined with BR's planned introduction and rolling stock cascade schedule, which was not aided by the mid-construction period privatisation of the builders, BREL, led to much national bad publicity. Deliveries soon exceeded a year late at great cost to all parties. The underbody equipment was mounted on a raft and this proved inadequate and required fitting of a redesigned larger replacement. Minor fractures also appeared in some welds, particularly in door frames. It has been a major operation between BREL and BR Regional Railways to have these faults remedied with minimised disruption to planned services. They have enhanced the 'Express' services around the system which the Classes 155 and 156 had proved could run profitably, and although availability is reasonable overall targets around 90% will not be achieved until at least 1995 on completion of the current rectification programme.

While all units of Classes 141–150 and 153–158 can operate with each other, subject to route and speed limitations of all vehicles in the formation, the categories 141–144 (Pacer), 150 (Sprinter), 153–157 (Super Sprinter) and 158 (Express) are designed for different services. Combinations of different categories on the same train have been common but should now be infrequent in normal service, although for the 1992 autumn season some 'mixed partnerships' were formed (ie six Class 158 + Class 156 and one Class 158 + Class 150) as the Class 158 units disc brakes are not very good at removing leaf mulch – another modification had a successful trial in the autumn of 1992; the fitting of scrubber blocks to Class 158s to clean the wheels.

Classes 141–150/1 have full width cab ends and are thus only gangway fitted between vehicles of the unit. Some Class 150/1 units have been semi-permanently formed with one coach of a Class 150/2 to form a three-car unit. All units of Class 150/2–158 have gangway connections through the whole unit which allows staff, catering trolley and passengers through the train, particularly helpful where trains join/divide en-route and parts may be crowded.

CLASS 141
DRIVING MOTOR STANDARD, DMS + DMSL, Codes DP2.28 + DP2.29
Built: BREL Derby 1983 [Leyland Bus bodies] (folding doors)
Engines: One per vehicle Leyland TL11 200hp
Maximum speed: 75mph
Business: North East (West Yorkshire PTE)
Number series: Units 141101-20, Vehicles 55502-41
Fleet size: 19 two-car units.
Vehicle length: 15.45m   **Weight:** 21t
Seats: DMS: 50, DMSL: 44   **Toilet:** DMSL: 1

CLASS 142
DRIVING MOTOR STANDARD, DMS + DMSL, Codes DP2.34 + DP2.35
Built: BREL Derby 1985 [Leyland Bus bodies] (folding doors)
Engines: One per vehicle Leyland TL11 200hp
Maximum speed: 75mph
Businesses: North East (42), North West 53)
Number series: Units 142001-96 Vehicles 55542-55641, 55701-92
Fleet size: 95 two-car units
Vehicle length: 15.55m   **Weight:** 25t
Seats: DMS: 62, DMSL: 59   **Toilet:** DMSL: 1

CLASS 143
DRIVING MOTOR STANDARD, DMS + DMSL, Codes DP2.34 + DP2.35
Built: Walter Alexander 1985 [Andrew Barclay underframes] (folding doors)
Engines: One per vehicle Leyland TL11 200hp, being replaced during 1993 by Cummins LR10 225hp
Maximum speed: 75mph
Business: South Wales & West
Number series: Units 143601-25, Vehicles 55642-91
Fleet size: 25 two-car units
Vehicle length: 15.55m   **Weight:** 24.5t
Seats: DMS: 62, DMSL: 59   **Toilet:** DMSL: 1

CLASS 144
DRIVING MOTOR STANDARD, DMS + DMSL, Codes DP2.40 + DP2.41
MOTOR STANDARD, MS, Code DR2.05
Built: BREL Derby 1986-88 [Walter Alexander bodies] (folding doors)
Engines: One per vehicle Leyland TL11 200hp
Maximum speed: 75mph
Business: North East (West Yorkshire PTE)
Number series: Units 144001-13 (2-car), 144014-23 (3-car)
Vehicles 55801-23 (DMS), 55824-46, (DMSL), 55850-59 (MS)
Fleet size: 13 two-car (DMS + DMSL), 10 three-car units (DMS + MS + DMSL)
Vehicle length: 16.60m
Weight: DMS/L: 24.5t, MS: 23.5t
Seats: DMS: 62, DMSL: 60, MS: 73
Toilet: DMSL: 1

CLASS 150/0
DRIVING MOTOR STANDARD, DMSL + DMS, Codes DP2.30 + DP2.31
MOTOR STANDARD, MS, Code DR2.02
Built: BREL York 1984 (sliding doors).
Engines: One per vehicle Cummins NT855R5 285hp
Maximum speed: 75mph
Business: Central
Number series: Units 150001/02
Vehicles 55200/01 (DMSL), 55300/01 (DMS), 55400/01 (MS)
Fleet size: Two three-car units
Vehicle length: DMS/L: 20.06m, MS: 20.18m
Weight: DMS/L: 35.8t, MS: 34.4t
Seats: DMSL: 75, DMS: 79, MS: 84
Toilet: DMSL: 1

CLASS 150/1
DRIVING MOTOR STANDARD, DMS +

DMS, Codes DP2.38 + DP2.39
Built: BREL York 1985 (sliding doors).
Engines: One per vehicle, Cummins NT855R5 285hp
Maximum speed: 75mph
Businesses: North West (18), Central (32)
Number series: Units 150101-50; Vehicles 52101-50 (DMSL), 57101-50 (DMS)
Note: 16 units operate with an extra vehicle, Class 150/2 DMS/L
Fleet size: 34 two-car, 16 three-car units (see above)
Vehicle length: DMS/L: 20.06m
Weight: DMS/L: 36.5t
Seats: DMSL: 68, DMS: 70 (some have small variations for local authority requirements)   **Toilet:** DMSL: 1

CLASS 150/2
DRIVING MOTOR STANDARD, DMSL + DMS, Codes DP2.42 + DP2.43
Built: BREL York 1987 (sliding doors).
Engines: One per vehicle, Cummins NT855R5 285hp
Maximum speed: 75mph
Businesses: ScotRail (16), North West (13), Central (14), South Wales and West (41)
Number series: Units 150201-85, Vehicles 52201-85 (DMSL), 57201-85 (DMS)
Fleet size: 76 two-car units (plus 16 vehicles with Class 150/1 units- see above)
Vehicle length: DMS/L: 20.06m
Weight: DMSL: 37.5t, DMS: 36.5t
Seats: DMSL: 73, DMS: 76 (some have small variations for local authority requirements)
Toilet: DMSL 1

CLASS 151
DRIVING MOTOR STANDARD, DMSL + DMS, Codes DP2.32 + DP2.33
MOTOR STANDARD, MS, Code DR2.04
Built: Metro-Cammell 1985 (sliding doors).
Engines: One per vehicle, Cummins NT855R4 285hp
Maximum speed: 75mph
Business: Stored out of use
Number series: Units 151003/04, Vehicles 55202/03 (DMSL), 55302/03 (DMS), 55402/03 (MS)
Fleet size: Two three-car units
Vehicle length: DMS/L: 19.98m, MS: 19.60m
Weight: DMS/L: 32.4t, MS: 32.1t
Seats: DMSL: 68, DMS: 80, MS: 84
Toilet: DMSL: 1

CLASS 153
DRIVING MOTOR STANDARD DMSL, Code DX2.03
Built: Leyland Bus 1987-88 as Class 155, converted Hunslet-Barclay with second cab and other modifications 1991-92 (plug doors).
Engines: One Cummins NT855R5 285hp
Maximum speed: 75mph
Businesses: North East (7), North West (13), Central (32), South Wales and West (18)
Number series: Units 153301-85; Vehicles 52301-35, 57351-85
Fleet size: 70
Vehicle length: 23.21m   **Weight:** 38.8t
Seats: 72   **Toilet:** 1

CLASS 155
DRIVING MOTOR STANDARD, DMSL + DMS, Codes DP2.48 + DP2.49
Built: Leyland Bus 1987-88 (plug doors).
Engines: One per vehicle, Cummins NT855R5 285hp
Maximum speed: 75mph
Business: North East (leased by West Yorkshire PTE)
Number series: Units 155341-47, Vehicles 52341-47 (DMSL), 57341-47 (DMS)
Fleet size: Seven units
Vehicle length: DMS/L: 23.21m
Weight: DMSL: 39.4t, DMS: 38.6t
Seats: DMS/L: 80   **Toilet:** DMSL: 1
Note: Units 155301-35 converted to Class 153 (see above).

CLASS 156
DRIVING MOTOR STANDARD, DMSL + DMS, Codes DP2.44 + DP2.45
Built: Metro-Cammell 1987-89 (sliding doors).
Engines: One per vehicle, Cummins NT855R5 285hp
Maximum speed: 75mph
Businesses: ScotRail (46), North East (27), North West (15), Central (26)
Number series: Units 156401-156514, Vehicles 52401-52514 (DMSL), 57401-57514 (DMS)
Fleet size: 114 two-car units (for peak summer operations some units may be reformed as three-car for ScotRail)
Vehicle length: DMS/L: 23.05m
Weight: DMSL: 38.6t, MS: 37.9t
Seats: DMSL: 79, DMS: 84   **Toilet:** DMSL; 1

CLASS 157
DRIVING MOTOR STANDARD, DMS + DMSL, Codes DP2.— + DP2.—
Due to be built: 1994/95 (plug doors).
Engines: One per vehicle
Maximum speed: 75mph
Business: ScotRail, Central
Number series: -
Fleet size: 50 two-car units
Vehicle length: DMS/L: 23.05m apx
Weight: DMS/L: 38t apx
Seats: DMSL: 79, DMS: 84 apx.
Toilet: DMSL: 1
Note: Subject to tender and Government approval.

CLASS 158
DRIVING MOTOR STANDARD, DMSL(A) + DMSL(B), Codes DP2.51 + DP2.52 (see note)
MOTOR STANDARD, MS, Code DR2.07
Built: BREL Derby 1989-92, aluminium body, air conditioning, (plug doors).
Engines: One per vehicle, Cummins NT855R1 350hp or 400hp* or Perkins 2006 TWP 350hp†
Maximum speed: 90mph
Business: Express services.
Fleet responsibility: ScotRail (46), North East (17 [three-car] + 43), Central (39), South Wales and West (37)
Number series: Units 158701-46 (ScotRail), 158747-97, 158798-158814 (three-car), 158815-62†, 158863-72*; 158901-10 (West Yorkshire PTE)
Vehicles: 52701-52872, 52901-10 (DMSLA); 57701-57872, 57901-10 (DMSLB); 58701-17 (MS)
Fleet size: 165 two-car, 17 three-car units
Vehicle length: DMSL: 23.16m, MS: 23.18m
Weight: 38t
Seats: DMSLA: 70, 72 (WYPTE), MS: 70, DMSLB: 78.
Toilets: DMSLA: 1, DMSLB: 1 with special facilities for wheelchair and disabled passengers, MS: 2
Note: ScotRail units are receiving a screened off area in the DMSLA vehicles for First Class passengers with other improvements. Seating revised to 1st 15, Std 51. BRB has not reclassified these as 'Composite' stock.

Many of the designs in use by this business are the same as those for Regional Railways (RR). To avoid duplication in such cases reference should be made to the RR section for additional information where Codes are marked '+'

CLASS 101
Built: 1957-59
Business: Thames

DRIVING MOTOR BRAKE STANDARD, DMBS, Codes DQ2.02+, DQ2.32*
Number series: 51208-25, 51432-45, 53310-14
Fleet size: 12   **Seats:** 49* or 52

DRIVING MOTOR COMPOSITE, DMCL, Code DP3.17
Number series: 51498-51503, 53265, 53322-32
Fleet size: 7
Seats: 1st 12, Std 46   **Toilet:** 1

DRIVING TRAILER COMPOSITE, DTCL, Code DS3.02
Number series: 54081, 54362-54402
Fleet size: 6
Seats: 1st 12, Std 53   **Toilet** 1

TRAILER STANDARD, TSL, Codes DT2.01*, DT2.28+
Number series: 59072*, 59091, 59110-17, 59306, 59530-40
Fleet size: 1*, 6
Seats: 61*, 58   **Toilet:** 1

CLASS 104
DRIVING MOTOR BRAKE STANDARD, DMBS, Code DQ2.05
Built: Gloucester RC&W 1957
Business: Thames
Numbered: 53540
Fleet size: 1   **Seats:** 52

CLASS 108
DRIVING MOTOR BRAKE STANDARD, DMBS, Codes DQ2.12*+, DQ2.13+
Businesses: Thames* (1), North London (5)
Number series: 51909-42, 53628*
Fleet size: 1*, 5,   **Seats:** 52

DRIVING TRAILER COMPOSITE, DTCL, Code DS3.10, DS3.11*
Built: 1958-1960
Businesses: Thames, (4), North London (4)
Number series: 54194, 54223-79, 54491-95

Fleet size: 6, 2*
Seats: 1st 12, Std 53   **Toilet:** 1

CLASS 115
DRIVING MOTOR BRAKE STANDARD, DMBS, Code DQ2.33+
Business: North London
Number series: 51654-76, 51855-78
Fleet size: 5   **Seats:** 74

CLASS 117
Businesses: North London (3 x 2-car), Thames (15 x 3-car, two x 2-car)

DRIVING MOTOR BRAKE STANDARD, DMBS, Code DQ2.20+
Number series: 51332-67
Fleet size: 22   **Seats:** 65

DRIVING MOTOR STANDARD, DMS, Code DP2.21+
Number series: 51374-51408
Fleet size: 20   **Seats:** 89

TRAILER COMPOSITE, TCL, Code DT3.05
Number series: 59484-59518
Fleet size: 15   **Seats:** 1st 22, Std 48

CLASS 119
Business: Thames
DRIVING MOTOR BRAKE COMPOSITE, DMBC, Code DQ3.02
Numbered: 51073/79
Fleet size: 2   **Seats:** 1st 18, Std 16

DRIVING MOTOR STANDARD, DMSL, Code DP2.03+
Number series: 51104/07
Fleet size: 2
Seats: 68   **Toilets:** 2

TRAILER STANDARD, TSL, Code DT2.16+
Number series: 59435/37
Fleet size: 2
Seats: 60   **Toilets:** 2

CLASS 121
DRIVING MOTOR BRAKE STANDARD, DMBS, Code DX2.01+
Businesses: North London (3), Thames (6)
Number series: 55022-31
Fleet size: 9   **Seats:** 65

SECOND GENERATION UNITS

As most NSE routes are electrified this business was somewhat late in introducing new style diesel multiple units. They were introduced to Chiltern Lines in the autumn of 1991, Thames Lines in the late spring of 1992 and should commence on West of England services early in 1993.

CLASS 159

DRIVING MOTOR STANDARD, DMSL: Code DP2.60

MOTOR STANDARD, MSL: Code DR2.09

DRIVING MOTOR COMPOSITE, DMCL Code DP3.22

Note: Units built as standard Class 158 units. Specification being altered to include First Class accommodation.

Built: BREL Derby 1992, aluminium body, air conditioning, (plug doors). Interior modifications prior to delivery by Babcock Thorn, Rosyth

Engines: One per vehicle, Cummins NT855R1 400hp

Maximum speed: 90mph

Business: West of England

Fleet size: 22 three-car units

Number series: 159001-22. Vehicles: DMCL: 52873-94; DMSL: 57873-94; MSL: 58718-39

Vehicle length: DMSL, DMCL: 23.16m, MSL: 23.18m

Weight: 38t

Seats: DMSL: 72, MSL: 72, DMCL: 1st 24 Std 28, (plus 25 vestibule tip up seats per unit)

Toilets: DMSL & MSL: 1, DMCL: 1 with special facilities for wheelchair and disabled passengers

CLASSES 165/0, 165/1* & 166†.

DRIVING MOTOR STANDARD, DMS: Code DP2.53

MOTOR STANDARD, MS: Code DR2.08

DRIVING MOTOR COMPOSITE, DMCL: Codes DP3.19, DP3.20

Built: BREL York 1991-92, aluminium body, plug doors. Class 166 to be built 1993 as Class 165 plus air conditioning

Engines: One per vehicle, Perkins 2006 TWH 350hp

Maximum speed: *Class 165/0:* 75mph, *Classes 165/1 & 166:* 90mph

Businesses: *Class 165/0:* Chiltern Lines, *Classes 165/1 & 166:* Thames Lines

Number series: Unit Nos: Two-car 165001-28, 165118-37*. Three-car 165029-39, 165101-17*, 166201-21†

Vehicles: *Two-car Class 165/0:* DMCL: 58801-22/73-78; DMS: 58834-55/67-72 *Three-car Class 165/0:* DMCL: 58823-33; MS: 55404-14; DMS: 58856-66 *Two-car Class 165/1:* DMCL: 58879-98; DMS: 58933-52 *Three-car Class 165/1:* DMCL: 58953-69; MS: 55415-31, DMS: 58916-32 *Three-car Class 166:* DMCL (two per unit): 58101-42; MS: 58601-21

Fleet size: Two-car units: 28, 20*; Three-car units: 11, 17*, 21†

Vehicle length: DMS, DMCL: 23.31m, MS: 23.18m

Weight: *Class 165:* DMS, DMCL: 37.5t, MS: 35.5t, *Class 166:* DMCL: 39.5t, MS: 37.5t

Seats: *Class 165:* DMCL two-car: 1st 16, Std 72; DMCL three-car: 1st 24, Std 60; MS: 106; DMS: 98 *Class 166:* DMCL: 1st 16, Std 72, MS: 96

Toilet: DMCL: 1

DIESEL ELECTRIC MULTIPLE UNITS
NETWORK SOUTHEAST

CLASSES 205/0 & 205/1*
Built: BR Eastleigh 1957-1959. Class 205/0 non-gangwayed, Class 205/1 experimentally gangwayed within unit
Unit Nos: 205001-33, 205101*
Fleet size: 15, 1* units
Maximum speed: 75mph
Businesses: Surrey & Berkshire (1), South London (10), West of England [Wessex & North Downs] (2), Kent Coast* (3)

DRIVING MOTOR BRAKE STANDARD, DMBS, Codes DB2.03 and DB2.04†.
Number series: 60100-08, 60110*, 60111-25, 60145-51†
Engine: English Electric 4-cyl 4SRKT MkII, 600hp
Traction motors: Two English Electric Type 824
Seats: 42† or 52

TRAILER STANDARD, TS, Code DH2.03
Number series: 60650-58, 60660*, 60661-78
Seats: 104

DRIVING TRAILER STANDARD, DTS, Codes DE3.01, DE3.02†, DE3.03≠
Number series: 60800-08, 60811-32
Seats: 1st 13, Std 50; 1st 19 Std 50†, 1st 13 Std 62≠   **Toilets:** 2

DRIVING TRAILER STANDARD, DTS, Code DE2.04
Numbered: 60810*
Seats: 76   **Toilets:** 2

CLASSES 207/0 & 207/1*
Built: BR Eastleigh 1962. Class 207/0 non-gangwayed, Class 207/1 two-car only gangwayed within unit
Unit Nos: 207001-17, 207101-03*
Fleet size: 4, 3* units
Maximum speed: 75mph
Businesses: West of England [Wessex & North Downs], Kent Coast (Marsh Link)*

DRIVING MOTOR BRAKE STANDARD, DMBS, Code DB2.05
Number series: 60126-42
Engine: English Electric 4-cyl 4SRKT MkII, 600hp
Traction motors: Two English Electric Type 824
Seats: 42

TRAILER COMPOSITE, TC, Code DH3.01
Number series: 60600-16
Seats: 1st 24, Std 42   **Toilet:** 1
DRIVING TRAILER STANDARD, DTS, Code DE2.01
Number series: 60900-16
Seats: 76

ELECTRIC MULTIPLE UNITS
INTERCITY

CLASSES 488/2 2-CAR TFH + TSH & 488/3* 3-CAR TSH + TS + TSH
Trailer units numbered in NSE (South) EMU series.
Built: BR Derby 1973, rebuilt from Mk2f hauled coaches 1984
Unit Nos: 8201-10, 8302-19*
Fleet size: 10, 18*
Business: Gatwick Express
Maximum speed: 90mph

TRAILER FIRST HANDBRAKE, TSH, EP1.01
Number series: 72500-09   **Fleet size:** 10
Seats: 41   **Toilet:** 1
TRAILER STANDARD HANDBRAKE, TFH, EP2.03

Number series: 72602-47   **Fleet size:** 46
Seats: 56   **Toilet:** 1
TRAILER STANDARD, TS, EH2.85
Number series: 72701-18   **Fleet size:** 18
Seats: 56   **Toilet:** 1

CLASS 489

DRIVING MOTOR GUARD'S LUGGAGE VAN, GLV, EX5.61
Built: BREL Eastleigh 1984 as conversion of 1958 Mk1 design EMU driving motor vehicles.
Business: Gatwick Express.
Unit numbers: 9101-10   **Fleet size:** 10
Vehicle number series: 68500-09
Traction motors: Two 250hp English Electric

REGIONAL RAILWAYS
25 Kv AC ELECTRIC MULTIPLE UNITS

CLASSES 303/0* & 303/1
Unit Nos: 303001-47/52-91, 303048*
Built: Pressed Steel 1959. Sliding doors.
Gangwayed within units.
* Preserved Glasgow 'Blue Train' at Shields
ETMD, original non-gangwayed style for
Charter duties
Fleet size: 47, 1*
Business: ScotRail
Maximum speed: 75mph
Vehicle length: 20.18m

**DRIVING TRAILER STANDARD, DTS, Code
EE2.06*, EE2.41**
Number series: 75566-75600, 75747-50,
75752*, 75755-75801
Seats: 56, 83*

**MOTOR BRAKE STANDARD, MBS, Code
ED2.01*, ED2.20**
Number series: 61481-61514, 61813-23,
61824*, 61828-67
Traction motors: Four AEI (Metrovic) 207hp dc.
Seats: 48, 70*

**BATTERY DRIVING TRAILER STANDARD,
BDTS, Code EF2.02*, EF2.17**
Number series: 75601-34, 75803-06, 75808*,
75809-57
Seats: 56, 83*

CLASS 304
Unit Nos: 304002-43   **Fleet size:** 26
Built: BR Wolverton 1960-61, Mk1 design.
Non-gangwayed. Introduced as four-car
units, TC coach since condemned.
Businesses: North West (16), Central (10)
Maximum speed: 75mph

**DRIVING TRAILER BRAKE STANDARD,
DTBS, Code EG2.02, EG2.03**
Number series: 75646-78, 75858-65
Length: 20.31m   **Seats:** 82

**MOTOR BRAKE STANDARD, MBS, Code
ED2.03, ED2.15***
Number series: 61046-59*, 61629-46,
61873-80
Traction motors: Four AEI (BTH) 207hp dc.
Length: 20.17m   **Seats:** 72, 82*

**BATTERY DRIVING TRAILER STANDARD,
BDTS, Code EF2.03, EF2.04***
Number series: 75046-59, 75681-98*,
75868-75*
Length: 20.31m
Seats: 80   **Toilets:** 2

CLASS 305/2
Unit Nos: 305501-19
Built: BR Doncaster 1960, Mk1 design.
Gangwayed within units. Introduced as
four-car units, North West fleet now three-
car without TS vehicle.
Business and fleet size: ScotRail: (four-car)
305501/02/08/17/19 = 5
North West: (3 x four-car from May 1993)
305503/04/06/07/09/10/11/13/15/16/18 =11
Maximum speed: 75mph

**DRIVING TRAILER STANDARD, DTS, Code
EE2.20**
Number series: 75443-61
Length: 19.88m   **Seats:** 88

TRAILER STANDARD, TS, Code EH2.23
Number series: 70356-74
Length: 20.18m
Seats: 86   **Toilets:** 2
Note: Three stored vehicles will be returned to
traffic in May 1993 for short-term use on new
Manchester Airport services.

**MOTOR BRAKE STANDARD, MBS, Code
ED2.16**
Number series: 61410-28
Traction motors: Four GEC 200hp dc.
Length: 20.18m   **Seats:** 76

**BATTERY DRIVING TRAILER STANDARD,
BDTS, Code EF2.-**
Number series: 75424-42
Length: 19.88m   **Seats:** 80

CLASS 310/1
Unit Nos: 310101-11   **Fleet size:** 11
Built: BR Derby 1965, Mk2 design.
Gangwayed within units.
Business: Central
Maximum speed: 75mph   **Length:** 20.18m

**BATTERY DRIVING TRAILER STANDARD,
BDTS, Code EF2.11**
Number series: 76132-74
Seats: 80   **Toilets:** 2

**MOTOR BRAKE STANDARD, MBS, Code
ED2.19**
Number series: 62073-62115
Traction motors: Four English Electric 270hp
dc.
Seats: 70

TRAILER STANDARD, TS, Code EH2.32
Number series: 70733-75
Seats: 98

DRIVING TRAILER STANDARD, DTS, Code EE2.37
Number series: 76182-76224
Seats: 75   **Toilets:** 2
(Other vehicles in numerical sequence in NSE Class 310/0 units)

CLASS 314
Unit Nos: 314201-16   **Fleet size:** 15
Built: BREL York 1979, Sliding Doors,
Standard inner-suburban design.
Gangwayed within units.emergency egress door in cab front
Business: ScotRail
Maximum speed: 75mph

DRIVING MOTOR STANDARD, DMS, Code EA2.06
Number series: 64583-64614 (two per unit)
Traction motors: Four GEC G310AZ or Brush TM61-53 110hp (ea)
Length: 19.80m   **Seats:** 68
TRAILER STANDARD, PANTOGRAPH, TSP, Code EH2.11
Number series: 71450-65   **Seats:** 76

CLASS 318
Unit Nos: 318250-70   **Fleet size:** 21
Built: BREL York 1986, Sliding doors.
Standard outer-suburban design.
Gangwayed throughout.
Business: ScotRail
Maximum speed: 90mph

DRIVING TRAILER STANDARD, DTS, Code EE2.27 & EE2.28*
Number series: 77240-79, 77288/89 (two per unit)
Length: 20.13m   **Weight:** 29.6t*, 30.1t
Seats: 66* (with wheelchair space), 71 (one each per unit)

MOTOR STANDARD, MS, Code EC2.07
Number series: 62866-85/90
Traction motors: Four GEC G315BZ 350hp dc.
Length: 20.18m   **Seats:** 79

CLASS 320
Unit Nos: 320301-22   **Fleet size:** 22
Built: BREL York 1990, Sliding doors.
Standard outer-suburban design.
Gangwayed within unit.
Business: ScotRail
Maximum speed: 75mph

DRIVING TRAILER STANDARD, DTS, Codes EE2.38, EE2.39*
Number series: 77899-77920, 77921-42* (one + one* per unit)
Length: 19.95t
Seats: 76* (with wheelchair space), 77 (one each per unit)
Toilet: 1*

MOTOR STANDARD, MS, Code EC2.12
Number series: 63021-42
Traction motors: Four Brush 332hp dc.
Length: 19.92m   **Seats:** 77

CLASS 321/9
Unit Nos: 321901-03   **Fleet size:** 3
Built: BREL York 1991, Sliding doors.
Standard outer-suburban design.
Gangwayed within unit.
Business: North East (Leased by West Yorkshire PTE)
Maximum speed: 100mph

DRIVING TRAILER STANDARD, DTS, Code EE2.77
Number series: 77990-95 (two per unit)
Length: 19.95t   **Seats:** 78
MOTOR STANDARD, MS, Code EC2.16
Number series: 63153-55
Traction motors: Four Brush 332hp dc.
Length: 19.92m   **Seats:** 79
TRAILER STANDARD, TS, Code EH2.40
Number series: 72128-30
Length: 19.95t
Seats: 74   **Toilets:** 2

CLASS 323
Unit Nos: 323201-43   **Fleet size:** 43
Built: Hunslet TPL 1992-93. Aluminium bodied, plug doors. Gangwayed within unit. (Delivery commenced September 1992, service to commence Central in spring 1993)
Businesses: North West (17), Central (26)
Maximum speed: 100mph

DRIVING MOTOR STANDARD, DMS, Code EA2.72
Number series: 64001-22, 64023-25*, 64026-43. 65001-22, 65023-25*, 65026-43 (one each series per unit)
Traction motors: Four Holec three phase ac drives, type DMKT 52/24.
Length: 23.37m   **Seats:** 98, 82*
TRAILER STANDARD, TS, Code EH2.96
Number series: 72201-22, 72223-25*, 72226-43
Length: 23.44m
Seats: 88. 80*   **Toilet:** 1
Note: * Three units for dedicated Manchester Airport service.

REGIONAL RAILWAYS
750V DC ELECTRIC MULTIPLE UNITS

CLASSES 507 & 508*

Unit Nos: 507001-33, 508101-43*
Built: BREL York 1978-79, Sliding Doors, Standard inner-suburban design. Gangwayed within units. Emergency egress door in cab front
Fleet size: 32 + 1 stored, 40 + 3 stored*
Business: North West (Merseyrail)
Maximum speed: 75mph

BATTERY DRIVING MOTOR STANDARD, BDMS, Codes EJ2.02, EJ2.03*
DRIVING MOTOR STANDARD, DMS, Codes EA2.01, EA2.08*
Number series: BDMS: 64367-99, 64692-64734* DMS: 64405-37, 64649-91
Traction motors: Two GEC G310AZ or (some Class 508 only) Brush TM61-53 110hp (per vehicle)
Length: 20.20m   **Seats:** 74
TRAILER STANDARD, TS, Codes EH2.05, EH2.18*
Number series: 71342-74, 71483-71525*
Length: 19.92m
Seats: 82*, 86

NETWORK SOUTHEAST
25kv AC ELECTRIC MULTIPLE UNITS

CLASS 302/0

Unit Nos: 302201-30   **Fleet size:** 30
Built: BR Doncaster and York 1958-59, Mk1 design. Gangwayed within units.
Businesses: West Anglia (10), London, Tilbury & Southend (20)
Maximum speed: 70mph
BATTERY DRIVING TRAILER STANDARD, BDTS, Code EF2.01
Converted on refurbishment to BDTC, service now Standard Class only.
Number series: 75085-75100, 75190-75205, 75311-58   **Length:** 20.36m
Seats: 76   **Toilet:** 1
MOTOR BRAKE STANDARD, MBS, Code ED2.16
Number series: 61060-91, 61122/91-61226
Traction motors: Four English Electric 193hp dc
Length: 20.18m   **Seats:** 76
TRAILER STANDARD, TS, Code EH2.23
Number series: 70060-88, 70122/93-70226
Length: 20.18m
Seats: 86   **Toilets:** 2
DRIVING TRAILER STANDARD, DTS, Code EE2.19
Number series: 75033-79, 75236-83
Length: 20.36m   **Seats:** 88

CLASSES 305/1 & 305/3

Unit Nos: 305403-20, 305525-28

Fleet size: 8
Built: BR York 1960, Mk1 design. Non-gangwayed
Business: West Anglia
Maximum speed: 70mph
BATTERY DRIVING TRAILER STANDARD, BDTS, Code EF2.05
Number series: 75464-75511
Length: 20.36m   **Seats:** 92
MOTOR BRAKE STANDARD, MBS, Code ED2.04
Number series: 61431-80
Traction motors: Four GEC 200hp dc.
Length: 20.27m   **Seats:** 82
DRIVING TRAILER STANDARD, DTS, Code EE2.09
Number series: 75516-63
Length: 20.36m   **Seats:** 92

CLASS 306

Unit No: 306017   **Fleet size:** 1
Built: Metro-Cammell and Birmingham Railway C&W Co 1949 LNER design. Sliding doors, non-gangwayed. Preserved 'Shenfield' unit at Ilford EMUD
Business: Great Eastern - Charter use only.
Maximum speed: 70mph

DRIVING MOTOR STANDARD, DMS, Code EA2.03
Numbered: 65217

Traction motors: Four EE (Crompton Parkinson) 210hp dc.
Length: 19.24m **Seats:** 62

TRAILER BRAKE STANDARD, TBS, Code EJ2.01
Numbered: 65417
Length: 17.40m **Seats:** 46

DRIVING TRAILER STANDARD, DTS, Code EE2.11
Numbered: 65617
Length: 19.24m **Seats:** 60

CLASS 308/1
Unit Nos: 308133-65 **Fleet size:** 32
Built: BR Doncaster 1960, Mk1 design. Gangwayed within units.
Business: London, Tilbury & Southend
Maximum speed: 70mph

BATTERY DRIVING TRAILER STANDARD, BDTS, Code EF2.-
Built as BDTC, service now Standard Class only.
Number series: 75878-86/96-75919
Length: 20.18m
Seats: 76 **Toilet:** 1

MOTOR BRAKE STANDARD, MBS, Code ED2.16
Number series: 61883-61915
Traction motors: Four GEC 205hp dc.
Length: 19.88m **Seats:** 76

TRAILER STANDARD, TS, Code EH2.23
Number series: 70611-43
Length: 19.88m
Seats: 86 **Toilets:** 2

DRIVING TRAILER STANDARD, DTS, Code EE2.19
Number series: 75887-95, 75929-52
Length: 20.18m **Seats:** 88

CLASSES 309/1 & 309/3*
ESSEX EXPRESS UNITS
Unit Nos: 309601-08, 309612-27*
Fleet size: 8, 9*
Built: BR York 1962, Mk1 design. Gangwayed throughout
Business: Great Eastern
Maximum speed: 100mph
Vehicle length: 20.18m

CLASS 309/1
DRIVING MOTOR BRAKE STANDARD, DMBS, Code EB2.07
Number series: 61940-47
Traction motors: Four GEC 282hp dc.
Seats: 48

TRAILER COMPOSITE, TC, Code EH3.09
Number series: 71111-14, 71573-76
Seats: 1st 24, Std 28 **Toilet:** 1

TRAILER STANDARD, TS, Code EH2.27
Number series: 71107-10, 71569-72
Seats: 64 **Toilets:** 2

BATTERY DRIVING TRAILER STANDARD, BDTS, Code EF2.16
Number series: 75984-91
Seats: 60 **Toilets:** 2

CLASS 309/3*
BATTERY DRIVING TRAILER COMPOSITE, BDTC, Code EF3.05
Number series: 75638-67
Seats: 1st 18, Std 32 **Toilets:** 2

MOTOR BRAKE STANDARD, MBS, Code ED2.18
Number series: 61926-39
Traction motors: Four GEC 282hp dc.
Seats: 48

TRAILER STANDARD, TS, Code EH2.28, EH2.29†
Number series: 70254-59†, 71755-61
Seats: 64 **Toilets:** 2

DRIVING TRAILER STANDARD, DTS, Code EE2.29
Number series: 75970-83 **Seats:** 56

CLASS 310/0
Unit Nos: 310046-95 **Fleet size:** 38
Built: BR Derby 1965, Mk2 design. Gangwayed within units
Business: London, Tilbury & Southend
Maximum speed: 75mph
Vehicle length: 20.18m

BATTERY DRIVING TRAILER STANDARD, BDTS, Codes EF2.11, EF2.14*
Number series: 76130-79, 76698*
Seats: 80, 75* **Toilets:** 2

MOTOR BRAKE STANDARD, MBS, Code ED2.19
Number series: 62071-62120
Traction motors: Four English Electric 270hp dc.
Seats: 70

TRAILER STANDARD, TS, Code EH2.32
Number series: 70731-80 **Seats:** 98

DRIVING TRAILER STANDARD, DTS, Code EE2.-
Built as DTC (EE3.06), service now Standard Class only.
Number series: 76180-76229
Seats: 68 **Toilets:** 2

CLASSES 312/0 & 312/1*

Unit Nos: 312701-30, 312781-99*
Fleet sizes: 30, 19*
Built: BREL York 1975, Mk2 design.
Gangwayed within units.
Businesses: Great Eastern (35);
London, Tilbury & Southend (14*)
Maximum speed: 90mph
Vehicle length: 20.18m

BATTERY DRIVING TRAILER STANDARD, BDTS, Code EF2.13
Number series: 76949-74, 76975-93*, 76994-97
Seats: 84   **Toilet:** 1

MOTOR BRAKE STANDARD, MBS, Codes ED2.12, ED2.13*, ED2.14†
Number series: 62484-62509, 62510-28*, 62657-60†
Traction motors: Four GEC 270hp dc.
Seats: 68

TRAILER STANDARD, TS, Code EH2.09
Number series: 71168-71712, 71277-80
Seats: 98

DRIVING TRAILER COMPOSITE/ STANDARD†, DTC/S†, Codes EE3.05/EE2.-†
All built as DTC, LT & S service now Standard Class only.
Number series: 78000-48
Seats: 1st 25 Std 47; Std 72†   **Toilet:** 1

CLASS 313/0 & 313/1

Unit Nos: 313001-64   **Fleet size:** 64
Built: BREL York 1976, Dual voltage AC/DC units. Sliding Doors, Standard inner-suburban design. Gangwayed within units. Emergency egress door in cab front
Business: North London (7), North West London (13), Great Northern (44 [Six to West Anglia April 1993]
Maximum speed: 75mph

DRIVING MOTOR STANDARD, DMS, Code EA2.04

BATTERY DRIVING MOTOR STANDARD, BDMS, Code EI2.01*
Number series: 62529-92, 62593-62656*
Traction motors: Four GEC G310AZ 110hp (ea)
Length: 19.80m
Seats: 74

TRAILER STANDARD, PANTOGRAPH, TSP, Code EH2.10
Number series: 71213-76
Seats: 84

CLASS 315

Unit Nos: 315801-61   **Fleet size:** 61
Built: BREL York 1980. Sliding Doors, Standard inner-suburban design. Gangwayed within units.
Business: Great Eastern (47), West Anglia (14)
Maximum speed: 75mph

DRIVING MOTOR STANDARD, DMS, Code EA2.07
Number series: 64461-64582 (two per unit)
Traction motors: Four Brush TM61-53 or GEC G310AZ 110hp (ea)
Length: 19.80m   **Seats:** 74

TRAILER STANDARD, TS, Code EH2.16
Number series: 71281-71341
Length: 19.92m   **Seats:** 86

TRAILER STANDARD, PANTOGRAPH, TSP, Code EH2.17
Number series: 71389-71419
Length: 19.92m   **Seats:** 84

CLASSES 317/0 & 317/2*

Unit Nos: 317301-48, 317349-72*
Fleet size: 48, 24*
Built: BREL Derby & York 1981-87, Sliding doors. Standard outer-suburban design. Gangwayed throughout.
Businesses: West Anglia (33), Great Northern (39)
Maximum speed: 100mph

DRIVING TRAILER STANDARD, DTS, Codes EE2.16, EE2.24*, EE2.25†, EE2.32≠, EE2.35§
Number series: 77000-47, 77048-83§, 77084-95≠, 77200-19/80-83*, 77220-39/84-87† (two per unit)
Length: 20.13m
Seats: 70†, 71≠, (with wheelchair and secure mail area), 74

MOTOR STANDARD, MS, Codes EC2.02, EC2.05*
Number series: 62661-94, 62695-62708, 62846-65/86-89*
Traction motors: Four GEC G315AZ 332hp dc.
Length: 20.18m
Seats: 79

TRAILER COMPOSITE, TC, Codes EH3.07, EH3.08†*
Number series: 71577-71610, 71611-24†, 71734-53/62-65*
Length: 20.18m
Seats: 1st 22, Std 46
Toilets: 2

CLASSES 319/0 & 319/1*
THAMESLINK UNITS

Unit Nos: 319001-60, 319161-86*
Fleet sizes: 60, 26*
Built: BREL York 1987, 1990*. Dual voltage AC/DC. Sliding doors. Standard outer-suburban design. Gangwayed within unit.
Business: Thameslink (South London 17, Midland 69)
Maximum speed: 100mph
Vehicle length: 20.18m

BATTERY DRIVING TRAILER STANDARD, BDTS, Code EE2.34
Number series: 77290-77380, 77430-56 (even numbers only)
Seats: 78 (with wheelchair and secure mail area)

BATTERY DRIVING TRAILER COMPOSITE, BDTC, Code EE3.10*
Number series: 77459-97, 77973-83 (odd numbers only)
Seats: 1st 28, Std 37

MOTOR STANDARD, MS, Codes EC2.09, EC2.14*
Number series: 62891-62936, 62961-74, 63043-62/93-98*
Traction motors: Four GEC G315BZ 332hp
Seats: 79*, 81

TRAILER STANDARD, TS, Codes EH2.34, EH2.38*
Number series: 71772-71817, 71866-79, 71929-48/79-84*
Seats: 74*, 76   **Toilets:** 2

DRIVING TRAILER STANDARD, DTS, Codes EE2.33, EE2.40*
Number series: 77291-77381, 77431-57 (odd numbers only), 77458-96*, 77976-84* (even numbers only)
Seats: 78*, 81

CLASSES 321/3, 321/4* & 322†:
† STANSTED EXPRESS UNITS.

Unit Nos: 321301-66, 321401-48*, 322481-85†
Built: BREL York 1990, Sliding doors. Standard outer-suburban design. Gangwayed within unit. Unit 321425 modified with experimental air-conditioning system.
Fleet size: 66, 48*, 5†
Business: Great Eastern (62, 8*), North West London (40*), West Anglia (5†)
Maximum speed: 100mph

BATTERY DRIVING TRAILER STANDARD, BDTS, Codes EE2.36, EE2.42†

Number series: 77853-78, 77943-72*, 77985-89, 78274-79*, 78280-99, 78300-11*
Length: 19.95m   **Seats:** 65†, 78

MOTOR STANDARD, MS, Codes EC2.10, EC2.15†
Number series: 62975-63020, 63062-93*, 63099-104*, 63105-24, 63125-36*, 63137-41†,
Traction motors: Four Brush 332hp dc.
Length: 19.92m   **Seats:** 70†, 79

TRAILER STANDARD, TS, Code EH2.35, EH2.39†
Number series: 71880-71925, 71949-78*, 71986-90*, 71991-71210, 72011-22*, 72023-27†
Length: 19.92m
Seats: 60†, 74   **Toilets:** 2

DRIVING TRAILER COMPOSITE, DTC, Codes EE3.08, EE3.09*, EE3.13†
Number series: 78049-94, 78095-78130*, 78131-50, 78151-62*, 78163-67†
Length: 19.95m
Seats: 1st 35, Std 22†; 1st 16, Std 56; 1st 28, Std 40*

CLASS 341

Proposed new units for CrossRail 2000 (Shenfield–Liverpool Street–Paddington–Heathrow Airport/ Reading/Aylesbury). It is planned to introduce these from 1997 on Great Eastern lines to cascade units to other lines and withdraw life expired stock. Project awaiting Government approval

CLASS 371

Proposed new units for Thameslink 2000 (Peterborough/King's Lynn–King's Cross–London Bridge–Portsmouth/Ramsgate). It is planned to introduce these dual voltage units to existing services in advance of the new King's Cross station and route expansion in the London Bridge area. Project awaiting Government approval.

Opposite A Class 159 passes Salisbury Tunnel junction with the 1105 Salisbury to Basingstoke shuttle on 3rd April 1993. *Chris Wilson*

CLASS 405 4-SUB
(DMBS + TS + TS + DMBS)
Unit No: 4732 **Fleet size:** 1
Built: Southern Railway, Eastleigh 1948
Business: Preserved for Charter use
Maximum speed: 75mph
DRIVING MOTOR BRAKE SECOND, DMBS, Code EB2.65
Number series: 12795/96
Traction motors: Two English Electric dc
250hp (each)
Length: 19.05m **Seats:** 82
TRAILER STANDARD, TS, Codes EH2.63, EH2.66*
Number series: 10239*, 12345
Length: 18.90m **Seats:** 102, 120*

CLASSES 411/4 & 411/5 4-CEP
(DMS + TBC + TS + DMS)
CLASS 412/3 4-BEP
(DMS + TBC + TRBS + DMS)
Unit Nos: Class 411/4: 1501-05; **Fleet size:** 5
Class 411/5: 1507-1621; **Fleet size:** 115
Class 412/3: 2301-07; **Fleet size:** 7
Built: BR Mk1 design.
Class 411: BR Eastleigh 1956-61
Class 412: BR Eastleigh 1961
Businesses: Class 411: Kent Coast,
Class 412: Surrey and Berkshire
Maximum speed: 90mph
Vehicle length: 20.34m
Note: Vehicle numbers are listed en-bloc as
renumbering of units at refurbishment was
effected in the order of overhaul
DRIVING MOTOR STANDARD, DMS, Codes EA2.63, EA2.64
Number series: 61033-44, 61229-40, 61304-
61409, 61694-61741, 61762-61870,
61948-59 (two per unit)
Traction motors: Two English Electric
250hp dc (each) **Seats:** 64
TRAILER BRAKE COMPOSITE, TBC, Code EJ3.61
Number series: 70037-44, 70235-40,
70303-60, 70555-70610, 70653-59
Seats: 1st 24, Std 6 **Toilets:** 2
TRAILER STANDARD, TS, Codes EH2.82, EH2.84
Number series: 70033-36, 70229/30/41,
70260-70301, 70503-51, 70660-66,
71625-36, 71711/12
Seats: 64 **Toilets:** 2

TRAILER BUFFET STANDARD, TRBS, Code EN2.61
Number series: 69341-47
Weight: 35.5t
Seats: 33 **Toilet:** 1

CLASSES 413/2 & 413/3 & 413/4†
4-CAP (DTC + DMBS + DMBS + DTS,
† DMBS + DTS + DTS + DMBS)
Unit Nos: Class 413/2: 3201-11; **Fleet size:** 8
Class 413/3*: 3301-11; **Fleet size:** 8
Class 413/4*†: 3321-25; **Fleet size:** 5
Built: BR Mk1 design. BR Eastleigh 1957-58.
Formed by pairing Class 414 units,
declassifying First Class in one/† both DTC
vehicles. Non Gangwayed. Driving
equipment isolated on vehicles now
formed in centre of units
Note: Vehicle numbers in the three series
shown and declassified coaches are not in unit
number sequence.
Business: Kent Link
Maximum speed: 90mph

DRIVING TRAILER COMPOSITE, DTC, Codes EE3.61, EE3.62*
DRIVING TRAILER STANDARD, DTS, Codes EE2.21, EE2.22*
Number series: 75361-75417*, 77115-50
Length: 20.44m
Seats: DTC: 1st 19, Std 50; DTS: 69
Toilets: 2
MOTOR BRAKE STANDARD, DMBS, Codes EB2.69, EB2.70*
Number series: 61241-61303*, 65393-65429
(Two per unit)
Traction motors: Two English Electric
250hp dc each)
Length: 20.04m **Seats:** 84

CLASS 414/3 2-HAP (DMBS + DTC)
Unit Nos: 4308-14 **Fleet size:** 5
Built: BR Mk1 design. BR Eastleigh 1958.
Non-gangwayed
Businesses: Kent Coast
Maximum speed: 90mph
DRIVING MOTOR BRAKE STANDARD, MBS, Codes EB2.70
Number series: 61275-94
Traction motors: Two English Electric
250hp dc (each)
Length: 20.04m **Seats:** 84

**DRIVING TRAILER COMPOSITE, DTC,
Codes EE3.62**
Number series: 75395-75414
Length: 20.44m
Seats: 1st 19, Std 50
Toilets: 2

CLASSES 415/1 & 415/4 4-EPB
(DMBS + TS + TS + DMBS)

Unit Nos: *Class 415/1:* 5001 (preserved [p]),
5124-5280; **Fleet size:** 25 + 1 p
Class 415/4 (refurbished)*: 5401-97;
Fleet size: 78

Built: Southern Railway Eastleigh 1951-59.
Non Gangwayed.† Three DMBS from BR
Eastleigh 1957 stock now used in these
units.

Businesses: South London (4*),
Kent Link (25, 74* + 1p)

Maximum speed: 75mph
Note: Vehicle numbers are listed en-bloc as
renumbering of units was not effected in the
order of original build

**DRIVING MOTOR BRAKE STANDARD,
DMBS, Codes EB2.66, EB2.69†, EB2.77*,
EB2.78***

Number series: 14001/02(p), 14003-14104,
14207-14570, 65300-83† (Two per unit)

Traction motors: Two English Electric
250hp dc (each)

Length: 19.23m, 20.23m†   **Seats:** 82, 84†

**TRAILER STANDARD, TS, Codes EH2.68(p),
EH2.70, EH2.79*, EH2.80*, EH2.81*, EH2.82***

Number series: 15002-77, 15101(p),
15104-15206, 15207(p), 15208-15481
(Two per unit)

Length: 18.96m   **Seats:** 102, 120(p)

CLASSES 415/6 & 415/7 4-EPB
(DMBS + TS + TS + DMBS)

Unit Nos: *Class 415/6:* 5601-22;
Fleet size: 18
Class 415/7 (express):* 5623-28;
Fleet size: 6

Built: BR Eastleigh 1960. Non Gangwayed.
Business: Kent Coast*, Kent Link
Maximum speed: 90*, 75mph
Note: Vehicle numbers are listed en-bloc as
renumbering of units was not effected in the
order of original build

**DRIVING MOTOR BRAKE STANDARD,
DMBS, Codes EB2.71, EB2.72†**

Number series: 61520-61613 (even nos, odd
nos† – one each per unit)

Traction motors: Two English Electric
250hp dc
Seats: 84

TRAILER STANDARD, TS, Code EH2.71
Number series: 70379-70472 (Two per unit)
Length: 20.43m   **Seats:** 112

CLASSES 416/2, 416/3 & 416/4 2-EPB
(DMBS + DTS)

Unit Nos: *Class 416/2:* 6202-78 **Fleet size:** 43
Class 416/3:* 6301-34   **Fleet size:** 34
Class 416/4: 6401-18   **Fleet size:** 18

Built: BR Eastleigh 1953, 1955-59. Non
Gangwayed. Classes 416/2 & 416/4 to BR
Mk1 design, Class 416/3 to SR design.

Businesses: Kent Link, South London*
Maximum speed: 75mph

**DRIVING MOTOR BRAKE STANDARD,
DMBS, Codes EB2.69, EB2.77*, EB2.81**

Number series: 14283*, 14488*, 14542-90*,
65301-92

Traction motors: Two English Electric
250hp dc

Length: 19.10*, 20.03m   **Seats:** 82 or 84

**DRIVING TRAILER STANDARD, DTS, Codes
EE2.64, EE2.69*, EE2.71†, EE2.74†**

Number series: 16101-34*, 77113,
77501-77

Length: 19.10*, 20.44m
Seats: 92*†, 94 or 102

CLASSES 421 4-CIG, 422 4-BIG*
(DTC + MBS + TS + DTC)
(DTC + MBS + TRBS + DTC)*

Unit Nos: *Class 421/3:* 1701-53 **Fleet size:** 53
Class 421/4: 1801-13, 1831-91
Fleet size: 68
Class 421/5: 1301-22   **Fleet size:** 22
Class 422/2: 2203-10   **Fleet size:** 7
Class 422/3: 2251-62   **Fleet size:** 12

Built: *Class 422/2:* BR York 1965;
Class 422/3: BREL York 1970
BR Mk1 design, Gangwayed throughout.
Classes 421/3 and 421/4 refurbished
specification. Class 421/5 refurbished
PORTSMOUTH GREYHOUND
specification.Classes 422/2 and 422/3
refurbished specification with TRBS

Businesses: Sussex Coast (421/3, 422/2,
422/3 - all; 421/4 - 35), Surrey & Berkshire
(421/4 - 18; 421/5 - all), Kent Coast
(421/4 - 13)

Maximum speed: 90mph, 421/5: 95mph
Vehicle length: 20.19m

DRIVING TRAILER COMPOSITE, DTC, Code EE3.69
Number series: 76022-76175, 76561-76639, 76718-76860
Seats: 1st 18 Std 36   **Toilets:** 2

MOTOR BRAKE STANDARD, MBS, Code ED2.64
Number series: 62017-78, 62277-62316, 62355-62430
Traction motors: Four English Electric 250hp dc.   **Seats:** 56

TRAILER STANDARD, TS, Code EH2.87
Number series: 70695-70730, 70968-96, 71035-71106, 71926-28
Seats: 72

TRAILER BUFFET STANDARD, TRBS, Code EN2.60
Number series: 69302-39   **Seats:** 40

CLASSES 423/0 & 423/1 4-VEP
(DTC + MBS + TS + DTC)
Unit Nos: Class 423/0: 3001-3194;
                         Fleet size: 73
Class 423/1: (refurbished, additional seating) 3404-3535   **Fleet size:** 116
Built: BR Mk1 design. BR Derby and York 1967-74
Businesses: [423/0 + 423/1] Kent Coast (32 + 29), Sussex Coast (8 + 38), Surrey & Berkshire (33 + 49)
Maximum speed: 90mph
Vehicle length: 20.18m
Note: Vehicle numbers are listed en-bloc as renumbering of units at refurbishment was effected in the order of overhaul

DRIVING TRAILER COMPOSITE, DTC, Codes EE3.65*, EE3.66†, EE3.67≠, EE3.68, EE3.71, EE3.73
Number series: 76230-69, 76335-76402, 76441-76560, 76641-76716, 76729, 76861-76942 (two per unit)
Seats: 1st 18, Std 46; 1st 24 Std 34†; 1st 24, Std 38*≠   **Toilet:** 1

MOTOR BRAKE STANDARD, MBS, Codes ED2.61, ED2.62, ED2.63
Number series: 62121-40, 62182-62271, 62321-54, 62435-75
Traction motors: Four English Electric 250hp dc (each)
Seats: Class 423/0: 58; Class 423/1: 76

TRAILER STANDARD, TS, Codes EH2.76, EH2.78*, EH2.83
Number series: 70781-70800, 70875-71034, 71115-71155   **Seats:** 90*, 98

CLASS 438 4-TC
(DTS + TC + TBS + DTS)
Unit Nos: 410, 417   **Fleet size:** 2
Built: BR York 1966. BR Mk1 design. Non self-propelled. Gangwayed throughout.
Maximum speed: 90mph
Business: Solent and Sarum (operated by NSE Charter unit)
Vehicle length: 22.15m

DRIVING TRAILER STANDARD, DTS, Code EE2.66
Number series: 76287-76302   **Seats:** 64

TRAILER COMPOSITE, TC, Code EH3.–
Number series: 70859-60
Seats: 1st 36, Std 8

TRAILER BRAKE STANDARD, TBS, Code EJ2.60
Number: 70812-26
Seats: 32   **Toilet:** 1

CLASS 442 5-WES
(DTF + TS + MBLS + TS + DTS)
WESSEX ELECTRICS
Unit Nos: 2401-24   **Fleet size:** 24
Built: BREL Derby 1987. Mk3 design, plug doors, gangway throughout.
Maximum speed: 100mph
Business: Solent and Sarum
Vehicle length: 23.15m

DRIVING TRAILER FIRST, DTF, Code EE1.60
Number series: 77382-77405   **Seats:** 50

TRAILER STANDARD, TS, Codes EH2.88, EH2.89*
Number series: 71818-41, 71842-65*
Seats: 78* (plus wheelchair point), 80
Toilets: 2

MOTOR BRAKE LOUNGE STANDARD, MBLS, Code ED2.65
Number series: 62937-60
Traction motors: Four English Electric 365hp EE546
Seats: 14 plus lounge bay seats

DRIVING TRAILER STANDARD, DTS, Code EE2.73
Number series: 77406-29
Seats: 78   **Toilet:** 1

CLASSES 455/7, 455/8 & 455/9 4-HIT
(DTS + MS + TS + DTS):
Unit Nos: 5701-42/50, 5800 (3-car), 5801-27/29-74, 5901-20
Built: BREL York 1977-80†/1982-85. Sliding Doors. Standard inner-suburban design. Gangwayed within units.

Fleet size: 137
Businesses: South London (46), Surrey and
Berkshire (91)
Maximum speed: 75mph
Vehicle length: 19.92m
**DRIVING TRAILER STANDARD, DTS, Codes
EE2.18, EE2.26**
Number series: 77579-77853 (Two per unit)
Seats: 74
**MOTOR STANDARD, MS, Codes EC2.03,
EC2.06**
Number series: 62709-62845
Traction motors: Four GEC 507-20J 205hp
Seats: 84
**TRAILER STANDARD, TS, Codes EH2.19†,
EH2.21, EH2.24, EH2.63***
Number series: 67400*, 71526-68†, 71637-
71710, 71714-33
Length: 20.18m   **Seats:** 84
Note: Vehicle 67400 former Class 210 vehicle
temporarily in unit 5918

CLASS 465: 2-Car (DMS + BDTS)
Unit Nos: 465001-24   **Fleet size:** 24
Built: BREL York 1991, Sliding doors.
Standard suburban design.
Gangwayed within unit.
Business: South London
Maximum speed: 75mph
**DRIVING MOTOR STANDARD, DMS, Code
EA2.67**
Number series: 64735-58
Traction motors: Two Brush 332hp dc.
Length: 19.92m   **Seats:** 79
**BATTERY DRIVING TRAILER STANDARD,
BDTS, Code EE2.76**
Number series: 78250-73
Length: 19.95m
Seats: 51   **Toilet:** 1

CLASSES 465/0 & 465/2
(DMS + TS + TS + DMS)
CLASS 466 (DMS + DTS)
NETWORKER
Unit Nos: Class 465/0: 465001-97;
                                Fleet size: 97
Class 465/2*: 465201-50; **Fleet size:** 50
Class 466/0†: 466001-43; **Fleet size:** 43
Built: ABB (BREL) York, 1991-94.
GEC Metro-Cammell*† 1991-93.
Gangwayed within unit.
Business: Kent Link
Maximum speed: 90mph
**DRIVING MOTOR STANDARD, DMS, Codes
EA2.68, EA2.69*, EA2.71†**

Number series: 64759-64858, 65700-99*
(two per unit); 64860-64902† plus 94 tba
Traction motors: Brush/GEC hp three-
phase ac (each)
Length: 19.96m
Seats: 86   **Toilet:** 1
**TRAILER STANDARD, TS, Codes EH2.92,
EH2.93≠, EH2.94*, EH2.95*§**
Number series: 72028-72126≠ (even
numbers), 72029-72127 (odd numbers),
72719-72817* (odd numbers),
72720-72818*§(even numbers) plus 94 tba
Length: 19.34m
Seats: 86† (with wheelchair point), 90
**DRIVING TRAILER STANDARD, DTS, Code
EE2..79**
Number series: 78312-54†
Length: 19.96m   **Seats:** 82

CLASS 482 2-car,
DMS + MS
Units Nos: 482001-10   **Fleet size:** 10
Built: ABB Derby 1993. Tube size stock,
generally to London Underground
Central Line design. Welded aluminium
extruded bodies. Externally hung sliding
doors.
Maximum speed: 60mph   **Length:** 16.25m
**DRIVING MOTOR STANDARD, DMS, EA2.70
MOTOR STANDARD, MS, EC2.20**
Number series: DMS: 65501-10,
MS: 67501-10
Traction motors: Brush/ABB 43kW dc on
each axle   **Seats:** 36
Note: Class 482 trains were expected to enter
service on the Waterloo & City line in replace-
ment of 1940-vintage Class 487s in summer
1993.

CLASS 483 2-car, DMS + DMS
Unit Nos: 001-009   **Fleet size:** 9
Built: Metro-Cammell 1938 for London
Transport. Rebuilt BRML Eastleigh 1989 for
BRB.
Maximum speed: 45mph
**DRIVING MOTOR STANDARD, DMS, Codes
EA2.65, EA2.66**
Number series: 121-29, 221-29
(One each per unit)
Traction motors: Two GEC 168hp dc each
Length: 15.94m   **Seats:** 42